Leicestershire
Edited by Lynsey Hawkins

First published in Great Britain in 2004 by:
Young Writers
Remus House
Coltsfoot Drive
Peterborough
PE2 9JX
Telephone: 01733 890066
Website: www.youngwriters.co.uk

All Rights Reserved

© *Copyright Contributors 2004*

SB ISBN 1 84460 364 4

Foreword

This year, the Young Writers' 'Poetry In Motion' competition proudly presents a showcase of the best poetic talent selected from over 40,000 up-and-coming writers nationwide.

Young Writers was established in 1991 to promote the reading and writing of poetry within schools and to the youth of today. Our books nurture and inspire confidence in the ability of young writers and provide a snapshot of poems written in schools and at home by budding poets of the future.

The thought effort, imagination and hard work put into each poem impressed us all and the task of selecting poems was a difficult but nevertheless enjoyable experience.

We hope you are as pleased as we are with the final selection and that you and your family continue to be entertained with *Poetry In Motion Leicestershire* for many years to come.

Contents

Abigail Bonshor 1

Abington High School
Laura Marriott (12) 1
Ruth Bowe (12) 2
Laura Smith (12) 2
Alice Brewin (12) 3
Sophie Boyd (12) 3
Andrea Casey (12) 4
Louisa Holland (12) 4
Matthew Osborne (12) 5
Gurpreet Sidhu (12) 5
Louisa Dovey (12) 6
Joe Houlihan (12) 6
Victoria Pring (12) 7
Emma Bailey (13) 7
David Griffiths (12) 8
Velisha Jethwa (11) 9
Sophie Collings (12) 10
Hannah Brookes (12) 10
Daniel Murphy (12) 11
George Wright (12) 11
Kay Morley (12) 12
Amy Rodwell (11) 12
Amie Lowes (12) 13
Beccy Crosby (11) 14
Lucy Brown (11) 14
Joseph Barker (11) 15
Ben Atkinson (11) 15
Kim Hoffman (13) 16
Beth Willars (11) 16
Fern Wright (12) 17
Lisa Crispin (14) 17
Jessica Buckby (13) 18
Cibié-Louise Brown (11) 18
Rheo Smith (12) 19
Sam Mills (11) 19
Hannah Chamberlain (13) 20
Carla Sibson (11) 20

Eve Morley (11)	21
Jenny Pollock (13)	22
Natasha Moran (11)	22
Adam Smith (13)	23
Matthew Sargent (11)	23
Jayleigh Stretton (13)	24
Jack Barden (12)	24
Kirsty Cooper (13)	25
Jaghit Sidhu (11)	25
Ami Aubrey (13)	26
Katie Smith Atherton (13)	27
Kelly Albert (13)	28
Jack Brougham (13)	28
Lois Harrison (13)	29
Shreena Bhatt (13)	29
Glenn Brookes (13)	30
Jaspreet Kaur Pattar (13)	30
Chris Irving (13)	31
Coco-Chanel Chauhan (13)	31
Jan Akerman (12)	32
Paul Smith (13)	32
Emily Wake (13)	33
Holly Arnold (14)	34
Tom Harris (13)	34
Rebecca Barker (13)	35
Natalie Hackett (14)	35
James Tipler (13)	36
Louise Griggs (14)	36
Harpreet Sehmi (13)	37
Tejal Solanki (13)	37
Sam Moffoot (13)	38
Natalie Spurden (13)	38
Joe Ladlow (13)	39
Samantha Houlihan (13)	39
Jake Wright (14)	40
Adam Gibbins (13)	41
Danni Palmer (13)	42
Tom Green (13)	43
Craig Appleby (13)	44
Kirstie Abbott (13)	45

Loughborough High School

Alice Hale (11)	45
Vaila Ormiston (11)	46
Elise Cole (11)	46
Victoria Smith (12)	47
Siobhan Sullivan (12)	47
Shreenal Ghelani (11)	48
Anika Karia (11)	48
Lucy Hagger (11)	49
Hannah Andrews (12)	50
Emma Haig (12)	51
Katie Gray (12)	52
Laura Mason (11)	52
Betsy Chadbourn (11)	53
Charlotte O'Connor (11)	53
Bernadette Ellerby (11)	54
Rosie Stafford (11)	55
Amanda Dalby (13)	56
Naomi Pakenham (13)	57
Nicole Turner (14)	58
Lauren Kluckow (14)	59
Francesca Smith (12)	60
Emily Wainwright (13)	61
Simran Chaggar (13)	62
Fiona Clegg (14)	63
Rebecca Williams (13)	64
Seneka Nakagawa (14)	65
Philippa Aspinall (13)	66
Helena Dean (12)	66
Louisa Ackerley (13)	67
Sophie Heffernan (12)	67
Rachael Beasley (13)	68
Becky Jackson (12)	69
Jaspreet Assi (12)	70
Charlotte Agar (12)	70
Katie-Rose Gilmore (12)	71
Hannah Taylor (12)	71
Georgina Kearney-Bambridge (12)	72
Meena Mistry (12)	72
Laura Baker (12)	73
Sophie Wheeler (12)	73

Sarah Grove (12)	74
Saanchi Sama (13)	75
Hannah Raban (12)	76
Gabby MacSweeney (11)	76
Sally Smith (12)	77
Toni Ashford (11)	77
Robyn Vitols (12)	78
Pooja J Thakor (12)	78
Catherine Hall (13)	79
Rebecca Lait (11)	79
Helen Cartwright (11)	80
Sophy Nash (14)	81
Catherine Sowerbutts (14)	82
Sarah Oatley (15)	83
Sarah Bowden (12)	84
Francesca Hicks (11)	85
Lorna Sowerbutts (11)	86
Emma Schofield (12)	87

Lutterworth High School

Jenna Lee & Jenny Turner (12)	87
Jodie Brightmore (12)	88
Peter Rowe (12)	89
Rebecca Amy Simpson (12)	90
Marcus Ikin (12)	90
Brittany Holland (12)	91
Oliver Van Allen (12)	92
Melissa Creese (12)	92
Melissa Sharpe (12)	93
Joe Seymour (12)	93
Natalie Cooper (12)	94
Elliot Hollingsworth (13)	95
Karla Bray (12)	96
Tom Taylor (13)	97
Sarah Edgington (12)	98
David Monk (13)	99
Laura Heath (12)	100
Jade Elliott (12)	101
Emma Weston (12)	102
Jemma Thomas (12)	103
Gemma Watson (12)	104

Daniel Smalley (12)	104
Harry Targett (12)	105
Callum Hall (12)	105
Matt Creasey (12)	106
Dan Liscombe (12)	106
David Mitchinson (13)	107
Ian Dowler (12)	107
James Hughes (12)	108
Natasha Buck (12)	109
Emma Cluley (12)	110
Natalie Roe (12)	111
Toni Wright (13)	112
Allen Carvin (12)	112
Anna Greiff (12)	113

Maplewell Hall Special School

Ricky Fryers (15)	113
Christopher Smith (15)	114
Eluned Bicknell (15)	114
Mindy Rakhra (15)	114
Louise Parker (15)	115
Paul Mattox (15)	115
Anne Marie Burrows (15)	115
Daniel Murrell (16)	116
Daniel Hewitt (15)	116
Robbie Jamieson (15)	116
Tom Styles (16)	116

Mount Grace High School

Carina Knox (13)	117
Anna Robinson (12)	117
Holly Kemp (13)	118
Sarah Shreeve (12)	118
Hannah Godrich (12)	119
Amy Tyrrell (11)	119
Nicola Roper (13)	120
Keira Miller (13)	121

Redmoor High School

Nisur Nadar (13)	122

Shepshed High School
Kerry Exon (11) — 122
Astin Storer (11) — 123
Cassie Soars (12) — 123
Chloe Jones (11) — 124
Ryan Locke (11) — 124
Rachael Burton (10) — 125
Chelsea Davies (11) — 125
Luke Eggleston (11) — 126
Georgia Bennett (10) — 126
Katie Hutchinson (11) — 127
Bethan Johnson (11) — 127
Christopher Davis (12) — 128
Georgina Wilson (11) — 128
Hayley Mabe (11) — 129
Neha Puntambekar (11) — 129
Sean Pell (11) — 130
Laura Francis (11) — 130
Siân Plummer (11) — 131
Lewis Brown (11) — 131

The Garendon High School
Seetal Patel (11) — 131
Charlie Craggs (11) — 132
Megan Spencer aka Kirk (11) — 132
Daniel Hurrell (13) — 133
David Mortimer (12) — 133
Daryl-Hannah Webster (11) — 134
Yasmin Mahboubi (11) — 134
Alana Spencer (11) — 135
Helen Jasmin Orr (11) — 135
Andrea Cooper (11) — 136
Joshua Davis (11) — 137
Oliver Turton (11) — 137
Belinda Edney (14) — 138
Sean Erskine (12) — 138
Jack Price (12) — 139
Roshun Lakha (11) — 139
Megan Griffiths (12) — 140
Andrew Danby Knight (11) — 140
Emily Brailsford (11) — 141

Layton Weston (11)	141
Vishantji Odedra (11)	142
Mark Boyde-Shaw (11)	142
Emma Peach (11)	143
Jade Hassall (11)	144
Ben Wall (12)	145
Antony Pyatt (11)	145
Hannah Bailey (12)	146
Stacey Hodgett (11)	148
Jordan Makwana (11)	148
Malick Attenborough (11)	149
Daisy-Mae Willumsen (11)	149
Elizabeth Green (11)	149
Rosamund Piper (11)	150
Denis Njiru (11)	151
Georgina Clayton (11)	151
Seven Bajot (11)	152
Danielle Mitchell (11)	153
Stefan Scutt (11)	153
Petra Baker (11)	154
Richard Squires (12)	154
Ajay Patel (11)	154
Kane McCaughie (11)	155
Jonny Nandakumar (11)	155
Kelly Spiby (11)	156
Laurence Vardaxglou (11)	156
Rachel Blanchard (11)	157
Scott Lacey (11)	157
Thomas Neill (11)	158
Charlie Hague (11)	158
James Langran (11)	159
Gemma Brailsford (12)	159
Sam Potter (11)	159
Emily Shaw (11)	160
Sophie Mayfield (12)	160
Rachel Edney (11)	161

The Grange School

Matthew Ayris (13)	161
Gary Bright (11)	162
Brett Bailey (12)	162

Matthew Snow (14)	163
Darren George (12)	163
Daniel Masters (12)	164
Ewan Bellamy (10)	164
Alex Franklin (15)	165
Michael Shaw (12)	165
Jack Makepeace (9)	166
Darryl Chambers (15)	166
David Haman (14)	166
Edmund Maile (13)	167
Jason Johnson (13)	167
Sam Duffield (14)	167
Stevie Newbold (14)	168
Dean Gray (12)	168
Liam Barber (14)	169
Marshyane Allen (12)	169

The Rutland College

Sarah Fowler (16)	170
Nicole Baines (16)	170
Kayleigh Smith (17)	171
Emily Culpin (16)	171
Ben Knight (16)	172
Gemma Willison (17)	173
Julia Penfold (16)	174
Katie Almond (16)	175
Harriet Moody (16)	176
Christian Aleksov (16)	176
Terri Lynch (16)	177
Loretta Johnson (16)	177
Coby Richardson (17)	178
Tori Thomas (16)	178
Charlotte Wilce (17)	179
Sarah Bruce (16)	179
Hazel Johns (16)	180
Hannah D'Cruz (16)	181
Russell Kent-Payne (16)	182
Graham Turner (16)	183
Kirsty Chuter (16)	184
Katie Folwell (16)	185
Dominic Tomes (16)	186

Vale Of Catmose College
James Barlow (14) — 186
Vicki Potter (12) — 187
Sophie Arnold (14) — 187
Daniel Goodwin (14) — 188
Caroline Kirstein (14) — 188
Katie Burton (14) — 189
Pippa Gray (12) — 189
Yasmin Mulligan (15) — 190
Hannah Arnold (12) — 190
Georgia Gibson-Smith (12) — 191
Lauren McCombie Smith (14) — 191
Kelly Pridmore (14) — 192
Luke Chase (15) — 192
Christopher Young (14) — 193
Tom Hampson (14) — 193
Rosie Hind (14) — 194
Simon Brown (14) — 194
Emily Wilce (14) — 195

The Poems

The Seaside

Every step she took her feet sank in the sand,
The cold sea made her toes tingle as it touched her feet,
Above her head, seagulls circled squawking noisily,
As her head lifted up to look at the white clouds, the salty air ran
                                                      under her small nose,
The sun shone on her golden hair and swayed in the small breeze,
All around her the children played and their laughs made her
                                                       warm inside,
She did not know if these feelings would last forever?

Abigail Bonshor

Today At 37.11

Today at 37.11
Mice will hunt cats through the fields,
The door will open you,
Today at 37.11
The sand tide will be in,
The stars will shine this morning,
Today at 37.11
Donkeys will ride humans on the beach,
Drivers will be walking their cars on the pavement,
Today at 37.11
Music will listen to us,
Lamps will switch us on,
Tonight at tea, dinner will eat me,
Tonight at 37.11
My pillow will sleep on me.

Laura Marriott (12)
Abington High School

Today At 37.12

Today at 37.12
A CD player will listen to you
Rock songs will be sung by rocks
Cheetahs will be caught cheating at Poker
Money will be placed all over the Earth but nobody will want it
George Bush will get a love letter from Saddam Hussein
Snow will come out in summer
Today at 37.12
Elephants will kill humans for their teeth
Our greens will eat us
Donkeys will ride humans on the beach
Stars will shine in the afternoon
The door will open to you
Cheese will eat mice
In the European countries cars will be driven on the pavements
and people will walk on the road
Fish will fly
Today at 37.12
The Channel Tunnel will fill with boats and the oceans with cars
Mice will hunt cats through the fields
Dogs will take humans for a walk
All babies will automatically turn 800 when born
All oranges will be purple and grapes orange
Poo will have a pleasant smell and be sold in air freshener cans
Cookers will freeze your food and fridges will be used for boiling milk.

Ruth Bowe (12)
Abington High School

Falling Leaves

The falling leaves
Swoop like a swift and summer's eve
Mounds of leaves
Gleam like piles of gold in the winter sunset.

Laura Smith (12)
Abington High School

What Am I?

I'm all shapes and sizes,
And colours galore,

But whichever it is,
I'll rest on the floor!

I'll never get fat,
If you fill me with food,

Some people will call me
A real 'cool' dude!

When I am empty,
You can give me some more,

And watch me light up,
As you open my door!

(A fridge.)

Alice Brewin (12)
Abington High School

The Sea

Deep, deep darkness of the sea,
An ocean bed of velvet-blue.
Shimmering in the sunlight,
Waves streaking by.

Glistening colours shining through,
Creatures swimming, big and small.
Shadows lurking in the deep,
Crabs and lobsters, claws held high.

Waves crashing on the sand,
Whispering waves washing up.
Fishes flowing with the tide,
In the oceans so clear and blue.

Sophie Boyd (12)
Abington High School

My Mum

When I feel down or tired in the day
You give me a boost and it's all ok
When I feel down you're always around
There to help me get up off the ground.

I hate it when we fall out, and you get sad
It's always my fault and I feel really bad
I wish I could change it, somehow, some way
But in the end, although it's my fault, you say it's ok.

Let's not forget we have loads of fun
The sort of fun for daughter and mum
We go out to parties and the fair
We get all dressed up, and you do my hair.

When people tell me their mums have died
It makes me feel all sad inside
I don't know what I would do if you weren't around
Who would be there to help me up off the ground?

Andrea Casey (12)
Abington High School

Autumn

Autumn's like a werewolf howling in the breeze,
He sits upon the mountain leaning on his knees.
His howl is like a gust of wind rocking trees from side to side,
When the leaves are flying high he'll run, pounce and glide.
When he's sitting on the mountain everything's quite calm,
But when he's howling on the ground always be alarmed.
His coat is like a field of grass where children go and play,
So when you're feeling cold in autumn,
Werewolf will learn some day.

Louisa Holland (12)
Abington High School

Fun In The Sun

Got up early!
It was dark.
We got in the car,
and drove so far.
Arrived on site,
in the daylight.
Picked our spot,
it cost a lot.
Put up our tent,
and paid our rent.
Went to the beach,
laughed and screeched.
We did have fun,
playing in the sun,
while flicking sand and digging.
Had an ice cream,
then I was keen,
to scare the seagulls away.
Back to our tent to have our tea,
then we all went to bed.

Matthew Osborne (12)
Abington High School

Darkness Is Running

Darkness is running
It's bumping and punching
'Help!' it shouts
A person or something lurking
Darkness meets its match
It turns all the trees into demons
It can't see what's in the shadows
It, shakes and . . . and . . .
It's a four-year-old running away from home.

Gurpreet Sidhu (12)
Abington High School

Springtime Birds

The springtime birds
Are out today,
On this fine morning
In sunny May.

With all their might
They sing to me,
With voices so
Joyfully.

Then one day
They don't appear,
As the winter days
Draw near.

As I sit in my
Rocking chair,
I gaze up at the
Empty air.

Louisa Dovey (12)
Abington High School

The Darkness

The darkness grows
Your imagination goes wild
You pray to God, don't let me die, I'm only a child
No one knows
As the darkness grows

You curl up in your sheet
And look where the curtain and wall don't quite meet
No one knows
As the darkness grows

Then you wake up and dread the next night
For the night before you had a terrible fright.

Joe Houlihan (12)
Abington High School

The Frost

Silently creeping, the frost
A silver cat face searching for family pride
Past the dark houses with grey doors
Searching for an open gate
Hackles up, it pounces
Finally finding its pride and joy
Through the open gate it sneaks
A welcoming sight to a hungry body
Creeping round the garden to find its prey
Not knowing where to start
It sees
It runs
It pounces
It's gone
Leaving its prey behind.

Victoria Pring (12)
Abington High School

Roller Coaster

The higher we go the more scared I get,
Hands shaking with fear,
Legs not able to stay still,

At the top we stop,
Then suddenly down we drop,
Upside down, around the loop,
Round and round,
Down we stoop.

At the end we came to a stop,
I enjoyed it so much I
Didn't know what I was scared of!

Emma Bailey (13)
Abington High School

Guitarist

Pick up my Gibson,
Pull on my strap,
Plug in the lead,
And turn up the amp.

Tune up the strings,
Get the right sound,
Pick a few notes,
Heart starting to pound.

With echo, delay,
Distortion and chorus,
Vibrato and wah-wah,
So much before us.

Remember the notes,
Strike the right chord,
Flexing my fingers,
Across the fret board.

Playing like Angus,
Like Eddie Van Halen,
James Heitfield, Kirk Hammet,
Rocking the nation.

The sound is amazing,
Electric and raw,
Tremendous, appealing,
Once hooked, there is no cure.

David Griffiths (12)
Abington High School

Tragic Magic

Round the back of the gigantic toy shop,
They've put an enormous skip.
Full of duff and broken stuff,
They're dumping at the tip.

It's where I found a magic set,
With Mark the other day.
The box was broken, some bits were lost,
But the wand was still okay.

I said to Mark, 'Wish you were a horse,'
I was only playing,
Next thing I knew he galloped off,
Round the car park neighing.

I wished him back, then I wished I was
A famous millionaire.
We wished for sweets and cakes,
And suddenly they were there.

I wanted most and so did Mark,
He pulled my hair, I called him names.
We had a fight and fell out,
No more playing games.

'I wish I'd never seen this thing!'
I cried and off it flew.
So just watch out if you find the wand,
It will do the same to you.

Velisha Jethwa (11)
Abington High School

My Grumpy Grandad

My grumpy grandad,
As grumpy as can be,
Likes to play a lot of golf,
And play fight with me.

My grumpy grandad,
Likes to watch TV,
Especially when the cricket's on,
It was his speciality.

My grumpy grandad,
Likes to moan and groan,
When you play a game with him,
The rules are always his own.

My grumpy grandad,
Has not a lot of hair,
He lost it a long time ago,
And now he doesn't care.

My grumpy grandad,
Is actually really lovely,
He spoils me to death,
And takes me on his holidays.

Sophie Collings (12)
Abington High School

Dreaming Chairs

School is finally over,
No one to sit on me,
No more times of thinking I'm going to collapse,
I feel ever so light and carefree.

No teachers that stand on me,
No more loud noises,
Well no more for at least . . . well I don't know,
I'm so happy because it's the summer holidays!

Hannah Brookes (12)
Abington High School

The Cinema

In bed no need to get up
I lay awake
Wondering what path this day will take.

Have breakfast,
A slice of toast,
An average breakfast, nothing to boast.

Go to the cinema,
Buy a seat,
Then I get something to eat.

Curtains rise,
Ads, what a bore!
But at the end of the film the crowd want more.

Daniel Murphy (12)
Abington High School

The Gate's Hopes

The gate was sealed,
Locked and bolted,
But it sincerely hoped
That it could be opened.

The gate felt forlorn,
Dirty and dusty,
Its metal features longing
For the touch of a human hand.

The gate was ancient,
Creaky and rusty,
Dreaming for a coat of paint
So it may stand with pride again.

George Wright (12)
Abington High School

Boys And Girls

Boys are strong, brave and rough,
they live to play football and act all tough.
Girls are pink, pretty and pink,
they dance all day, courtesy and blink.

If a boy was pink and as girl was blue,
what in the world would their mum and dad do?
Buy a girl shorts and a boy a pretty dress,
scruff the girl's hair up and make it a mess.

Boys are strong, brave and rough,
they like to play football and act all tough.
Girls are pink, pretty and pink,
they dance all day, courtesy and blink.

The boy would have to dance and look pretty,
and the girl would have to be silly and witty.
Mud on the shorts, make-up on the dress,
the thing that's the same about them is . . .

. . .they both make a mess!

Kay Morley (12)
Abington High School

Clouds

They're big, fluffy pillows so cuddly as can be
They disappeared yesterday, completely gone.
They're hiding from me!
Today I'm looking up high into the sky,
They are running on their toes - don't ask me why.
Other days they're angry and high up in the air,
Then they cry, fade away and die.

Amy Rodwell (11)
Abington High School

My Class . . .

Laura wasn't at school today,
Robert wouldn't go away.
Katie was acting weird again,
Ryan was throwing pens.
Roseanna was getting into a muddle,
Michael went and jumped in a puddle.
Ruth was revising for a test,
Andre kept being a pest.
Casey was building a house of sticks,
Tom was building a wall of bricks.
Hannah wanted to go outside,
But Rishi cried.
Gurpreet was drawing pretty patterns,
Jacob was telling us what happened.
Stacey was putting on her make-up.
Ashley was drinking from a cup.
Louisa was playing with her brother,
Nathan was playing with the other.
April was brushing her wild hair,
Andrew was being a grizzly bear.
Anum was talking to everyone,
Jess was celebrating because he'd won,
Craig was singing to see how he looks,
Harriet was doodling on her books.
Lauren was skipping around the room,
Josh was saying, *'Boom, boom, boom!'*
Fern was playing a game for two,
Kishval said could he play too?
That is my class.

Amie Lowes (12)
Abington High School

Trolley

Wire, with wheels that roll on the ground,
Sometimes disappear never to be found.
We use them by day or play with them at night,
And when they are used never out of your sight!

Sit on, ride on, sometimes a crash,
They fall in the water - what a big splash!
Down with the bikes and the rest of the mess,
I'll bet there are loads - even in Loch Ness.

These things on wheels are clever you see,
And love to hide in a bush or tree,
City Councils hunt them as hard as they can,
To bring them back to the rest of the clan.

You push one way, they go another,
The joy or pain of child and mother,
To shop and not to have one would be a great folly,
Cos you can't get along without your supermarket trolley!

Beccy Crosby (11)
Abington High School

Rain

Its panes fill with water,
And others do too,
Waiting, waiting,
For it to trickle down the clear glass,
Making it foggy,
And then the tears of gloominess drop onto the ground,
Drip, drop, drip, drop,
And then it starts to cry so fast that the water rises
and makes salty puddles.
When finally it's happy again and bright as can be,
Its puddles of tears dry up,
Until it gets lonely, grey and gloomy again and once more
the panes start to refill with tears.

Lucy Brown (11)
Abington High School

A Brick Monster

A face with four eyes,
Square in shape,
When it's black,
Its four eyes close.

A noise sounds
And its mouth opens,
Big pieces of food
Squelching in its mouth.

One ear sticks out,
Round in shape,
Pointing to the sky,
Receiving signals from other planets.

Lots of groups,
Big and small,
Some stand out,
Above them all.

Joseph Barker (11)
Abington High School

The Lightning Is Crying

Think about lightning,
All those tears that come crashing down,
Scaring everybody,
But only wanting company,
Every time it shouts out,
Everybody runs inside,
All those tears coming down,
But still nobody cares,
Children say, 'I'm scared Mummy!'
'Well maybe the lightning is too.
He's just trying to find a friend,
He's just trying to make a friend,
A lot like you.'

Ben Atkinson (11)
Abington High School

Sadness

I feel the tear running,
Down my lifeless face,
I feel the hollowness,
Inside the ugly outer case.

I see the darkly shaded graves,
On a lonely lilac backdrop,
I see myself swoop into the caves,
Like a bat back from its hunt.

I feel the desolate thinking,
And the heart with its emptiness,
I feel the smile on my face crinkling,
Into a nothingness line.

I see the interior of my cover,
As I sit inside the warmness,
I see the ripped-up picture of my lover,
On the stillness of my bedroom floor.

Kim Hoffman (13)
Abington High School

Friends

Friends can be good, friends can be bad,
They all do something that makes us feel sad.
It's either knocking our pen or making us slip,
Or sharing their lunch with some juicy gossip.
Or falling out over something quite silly,
Like dresses or shoes or someone called Billy.
But you'll soon find out that friends are okay,
Because without your friends you can't get through the day.

Beth Willars (11)
Abington High School

The Fairground

The fair is here again,
Yippee, all the fair owners beaming.
Lots of children (and adults) screaming,
Yippee, the fair is here again.

The fair is never a bore,
The music booming in my ear.
It really is quite nice to hear,
Children shouting, 'More, more.'

Now there's silence,
Nothing to hear.
For the fair has gone,
For another year!

Fern Wright (12)
Abington High School

Fireworks

They ascend like sudden fiery flowers,
That shatter upon the night,
Then topple to Earth in burning showers,
Of crimson, blue and white.

Like buds too astounding to name,
Each prodigy unfolds,
And Catherine wheels commence to flame,
Like whirling marigolds.

Rockets and Roman candles make
An orchard of the sky,
Enchanting trees their petals shake,
Upon each gazing eye.

Lisa Crispin (14)
Abington High School

Loneliness

Alone, no one to talk to,
Alone, nowhere to go,
Where life is such misery,
Where time moves by so slow.

Alone she sits in silence,
Alone she yearns and moans,
Where walls are closing in on her,
Where no one hears her groans.

Alone the pain gets worse,
Alone, not one kiss,
Where every day is useless,
Where Heaven seems like bliss,

Alone the knife gets nearer,
Alone the screams sound dumbed,
Where dying is her sweet relief,
When will the angel come?

Jessica Buckby (13)
Abington High School

Fire

Fire
A fierce bull
Steaming smoke everywhere
Moving swiftly
With a hellish look
Spitting everywhere
Spit, spit
Fire
A deadly bull.

Cibié-Louise Brown (11)
Abington High School

Sport

Sport is great fun,
It can be done by you and me,
We all make choices,
As to which sport it will be.

You may use your skills,
To catch, roll or throw,
You may prefer a sport,
That's fast or even slow.

So whether it be football,
Snooker or PE,
Sport can be enjoyed by all,
Especially by *me!*

Rheo Smith (12)
Abington High School

Morning

When I wake up I'm yawning,
And groaning and moaning,
Then I start washing and rushing,
And dashing and prancing.
Next I go to school,
I start walking and jogging,
And running and sprinting.
When I get to school I start,
Working and talking,
And jotting and writing.

That is what I do in the morning.

Sam Mills (11)
Abington High School

Hope

It all started when I was ten
My life became quite different then
I kept it bottled up inside
But when I went to bed I cried

Sometimes I felt no one understood
Why I wasn't being the way I should
I felt left out and all alone
I wished I felt safe in my own home

All I wanted was a better life
But to do that I had to strive
Strive for comfort and strive for love
Not expect it to float from above

Then one day I realised that there was some hope
If I wanted to try, if I wanted to cope
I could tell myself that it will all be okay
Then I could deal with my troubles another day

So since then I've really tried
Although I've struggled, although I've cried
If the memories come back I look to the sky
I just keep my chin up and let them pass by.

Hannah Chamberlain (13)
Abington High School

The Sun

The sun is like a tiger,
His dangerous flame spreads across the land,
His golden jewelled eyes shine down on the world,
His blazing claws scrap the forests,
His untamed jaws cause terrible blazes,
His orange burning coat sweeps across the world.

Carla Sibson (11)
Abington High School

Shopaholic

I shop all day,
And I shop all night,
I shop for clothes,
And things I like.

I buy my clothes from H&M,
From woolly jumpers to jeans with a hem.
A hairbrush, a watch, a big teddy bear,
I buy lots of things for me to wear.

I go to lots of different shops,
To buy shoes, food and bike locks.
I buy stationery to use at school,
Because at school I want to be cool.

A T-shirt, some trainers, a mountain bike too,
Shopping's a thing that I like to do.
I shop for myself, my friends and my mum,
And for my grandfather, I buy rum.

I want to buy a mobile phone,
And also a big TV.
I buy my shoes from Brantano,
There are lots of shops for me.

A novel, a pencil, some flip-flops too,
Shopping's a thing for me and you.
I go shopping with my mum and my friends,
I am upset when the day ends.

Eve Morley (11)
Abington High School

Red

Everyone sees it,
It seeps everywhere.
Houses,
Offices,
Schools.
Comes in forms -
Lover's tiff,
To world wars.
Red, red, red . . .

Me and you,
Fred and Phil,
Politics,
Arguments,
Road rage,
So much anger in the world.
Why can't we be calm?
Red, red, white.

Jenny Pollock (13)
Abington High School

The Moon

Does the moon ever set?
Does it ever go to sleep?
It's round and yellow,
Like a really big cheese.
My mum says that there is a man on the moon.
I bet he turns it on every night.
Where does it go on the dawning day?
Does it hide behind the clouds,
Or does it hide behind the sun to cover up its ghostly glow?

Natasha Moran (11)
Abington High School

The Ego Bruiser

Screwed in,
Blue, sky coloured.
Well-used, but . . .
Never abused.
Liquid consumer,
And what an ego bruiser.
As I found out!
It's easy to handle,
And, as I again found out, it's good for enforcing scandal.
Silver flashes,
As across the white sea of lines it dashes,
To help you to ruin you, or to hinder you.

Delightful and dreadful views its discarded on the page.
It's broken my heart and bruised my reputation in so many ways.
It's left me as black as the night, and filled me with rage.

Stop and think what can it do for you?

Adam Smith (13)
Abington High School

The Pen

Scarlet-red
Silver nibbed
Cartridge filled
Plastic and silver

The monster
Trails
Blue-black ink
Burns paper and whizzes
Through with all the ideas
People amazed at how fast
It burns papers.

Matthew Sargent (11)
Abington High School

No More Kitten

Tell us Mother about your mate,
Who got microwaved after her owner's date.

The old cat, once a young kitten,
Who once fitted in a pocket, or indeed a mitten,
She thought of her friends, how long ago,
Her life had ended so,

Sitting in a chair,
Having not a care,
She heard the door open,
Came walking up to see,
If there was 'anything for me'.
She croaked out the words, feeling a hand on her neck,

How she was to have a shock,
Indeed 180 watts, there's no need to mock,
Crying and scratching, at a door, no more mice catching,

The lifeless body, limp,
The nose, pink as a shrimp,
Feeling stiff hair, burnt skin,
No more rubbing against a shin.

Falling from that height,
Nothing moving in the night,
Eight floors up, a balcony door's shut,

No more kitten.

Jayleigh Stretton (13)
Abington High School

My Motorbike

Booming on my motorbike
Swiftly down lanes
Going like a bullet
Headlights beaming on the dusty roads
With the wind blowing in my face.

Jack Barden (12)
Abington High School

Sadness

A dark, bitter force grows inside,
Like a piece of mouldy moss,
It causes deep, dark pain,
To whom it may contain.

This world is cursed,
With this horrible sight,
As we see many in fright,
Misery, mourn and mellow,
Are just some of the words,
That describe this suffocating madness.

So please, help me get rid of my sadness.

I don't know what to do,
No respect, friends or happiness too.
It seems that not much can be done,
Because I know that my illness
Doesn't just affect me,
But everyone.

I just want to be happy.

Please can't someone
Help me pelt this sadness
Away?

Kirsty Cooper (13)
Abington High School

November

Autumn's annual return,
Snow and cold crowd out November,
Wrapped birthday presents of every colour,
Holidays begin with happy thoughts,
And celebrations are made ready for the festival of lights,
The candles are made in every style and colour
And charity begins its wonders again.

Jaghit Sidhu (11)
Abington High School

It's Hard To Have A Brace

I am creeping across the playground,
Hoping no one spots me,
Walking very silently, starting to run now,
'Oi brace face, what are you doing?'

Everyone laughs,
Everyone stares,
Names are being shouted,
It's so unfair.

Names are being bellowed,
Shouted and screamed,
I wish I were invisible,
So I couldn't be seen.

People are still laughing,
All the rest gape,
People surround me,
It is so unfair.

Just two more years
Of name-calling,
Two more years of taunts, teasing and tears.

People are laughing,
Others are staring,
I want to cry,
It is so unfair.

The day has come,
The brace has gone,
I wonder who the next brace face is?
But it was worth it,
My teeth are now perfect,
My smile is great,
Now I am always smiling.

Ami Aubrey (13)
Abington High School

True Love

Every second of the day,
Every minute I wake,
I see my true love standing there.

With his big brown eyes,
And lovely soft hair,
I see my true love standing there.

His gentle, manly hands,
And his thin, smooth lips,
I see my true love standing there.

Like a knight in shining armour,
On his silky, white horse,
I see my true love standing there,

Could this be real?
I don't believe it myself,
I see my true love standing there.

My dreams have come true,
My true love comes over and says, 'I love you,'
My true love is no longer standing there.

He whispers softly,
And will always remain in my head,
But my true love is no longer standing there.

His spirit will always guide me,
And I will never forget,
The time my true love was standing there!

Katie Smith Atherton (13)
Abington High School

All In Fours

Yellow, green, red and blue,
Six, twelve, ten and two.
Pens, paper, scissors, glue,
Old, ancient, modern, new.

Knives, forks, a wooden spoon,
April, March, May and June.
Saturn, Earth, Mars, the moon,
Morning, evening, night and noon.

Cones, players, balls and bat,
Gloves, socks, coats and hats.
Birds, rabbits, dogs and cats,
Protein, vitamins, energy and fats.

Carrots, cabbage, parsnips and peas,
Flies, wasps, ladybirds and bees.
Butter, milk, cream and cheese,
Pardon, thank you, sorry, please.

Kelly Albert (13)
Abington High School

Horizon Riser

The elliptical figure,
Of an incandescent shape,
Slowly rises
Above the sharply cut skyline.

Light explodes, like shrapnel,
Filling the morning air.
The surrounding beauty,
Pristinely formed, emerges.

Silence . . .
Spreading like butter on toast.
Rarely experienced,
Why, I wonder?

Jack Brougham (13)
Abington High School

Grandparent

When all is gone,
I am alone,
I feel scared and anxious,
But then I hear your gentle voice,
And then the world turns bright.

I see those wise old eyes,
Shining into mine,
And know you'll never leave me,
Always, you stay by my side,
Keeping me safe from harm.

You comfort me when I am sad,
And make me feel warm inside,
You hug me tight and smile,
And hum into my ear.

You have been in the world,
A lot longer than me,
And seen some dreadful things,
But still you stay happy,
And just think of good things.

Lois Harrison (13)
Abington High School

The Ocean

The ocean is a pool of tears,
Tears of Heaven,
Heaven looking down on Earth,
Crying on the grief of others,
As happiness took over,
Life began a new home,
In the tears of grief,
Now the tears of joy!

Shreena Bhatt (13)
Abington High School

Moving House

We explored a hidden room.
The attic, where things got left.

Baby-blue bunk bed.
Action Man and Lego,
fighting it out in a black plastic sack.
Action men cars and trailers,
veterans of many battles.
An old lawn mower, once Grandad's,
no one had the heart to throw it out.

Old books.
Old cars.
Old baby trike.
Baby paddling pool,
Old go-kart,
A mist of memories settle
With the dust.

And I know I've got to grow up
But not today . . .

Glenn Brookes (13)
Abington High School

I Love You

I love you so much, my heart is sure,
As time goes on I love you more.
Your happy smile,
Your loving face,
No one will ever take your place.
I also love your eyes,
And I love your smile,
I cherish your ways,
I adore your style.
What can I say, you're one of a kind,
And 24/7,
You're on my mind.

Jaspreet Kaur Pattar (13)
Abington High School

The Countryside

Driving through the countryside
Daffodils spreading up the fence
Bumping over rusty cattle grids
Rattle, rattle, rattle.

Rapeseed rising beautifully in a field
Sheep hungrily munching on lime-green grass
Rabbits hopping over the road
Hop, hop, hop.

No litter to be seen
Not a cloud in the clear blue sky
People galloping on their horses
Clip-clop, clip-clop.

Squirrels running through the trees
Chestnuts falling on the ground
Birds swooping through the sky
Whoosh, whoosh, whoosh.

Time to go home
Back to the city
Pollution in the air
Litter on the ground.

Chris Irving (13)
Abington High School

Tears

Steaming along with buds so small
It runs quite like a waterfall

It's previously seen on Bambi the deer
On a bright day it's crystal clear

Although you need a shoulder to lean
But people don't want to be seen

When happy or sad, it's sometimes made
But for everyone it's a great aid.

Coco-Chanel Chauhan (13)
Abington High School

New Evacuees

What has changed?
The heartless orange brick walls,
The chimneys like battalions of soldiers,
To scenic streams and waterfalls,
To trails of stones and rolling boulders.

What has changed?
The lights blacked out lights when the sirens awake,
The times spent under stairs with mice,
To food full banquets, what to take,
To Sunday dinner, herbs and spice.

What has changed?
The bomb shelters for hours on end,
The poor children and a dad with no spouse,
I wish my mother was here to see,
The end of the war here with me.

Jan Akerman (12)
Abington High School

My Pencil Walking

What do pencils do?
They walk across pages to help you.
Pencils can walk or run,
I think they have lots of fun.

Pencils run every day,
If they had mouths they would say,
'I love walking across your page,
I would love to go and dance on stage.'

This is my poem about a pencil walking,
Pencils might even be talking,
My pencil is going back in its case,
And I know it will have a smile upon its face.

Paul Smith (13)
Abington High School

The Challenge

Life is like an athlete,
Racing in a race,
We always face new hurdles,
Sometimes we make mistakes.

We go up and then come down,
In this one short time,
But there are always others,
In spirit and in mind.

Each time we turn a corner,
We learn a brand new thing,
We have to rise to the challenge,
So we can be the king.

Life is the feeling of existence,
The being of everyone,
Going through emotions,
When you meet someone.

Some people really love their life,
They're achieving all the time,
But others feel their life's a mess,
And wish that things were fine.

In life we have to make decisions,
And take so many chances,
We have to have experiences,
With others in romances.

But when we're gone,
What are we?
Do we go to another place?
Or are we just a memory?

Emily Wake (13)
Abington High School

The Bully

I lie awake all night
Just staring at the ceiling
I see the moonlit sky through the curtains
Just dreading when the sun rises
When I get up I'm dreading the bully coming
I see him everywhere
Just staring
When the bell rings I run to my class and sit there with my eyes bright
When 3 o'clock comes
I run
I run along the path when he appears
Out of nowhere
He pushes me
Then takes my money and runs
I sit there crying
What will I do?

Holly Arnold (14)
Abington High School

My Home

My home	My home
Orange	Blue
Secure, warm	Sad, shameful
Red	Green
Warm, bright	Shameful, hateful
Yellow	Black
Bright, joyful	Hateful, disgusting
Pink	Brown
Joyful, cosy	Disgusting, sorrowful.

        Yet all the walls are white!

Tom Harris (13)
Abington High School

War Or Peace

Why is there war and not peace?
The never-ending arguing,
And constant disagreements,
It doesn't make sense to me.

Why is there war and not peace?
All the sadness, pain and loss,
Of innocent people's lives,
It just doesn't make sense to me.

But why is there war and not peace?
I don't understand why people want power,
What's going on in their evil, twisted minds?

Why is there war and not peace?
Can't we accept that people have different beliefs?
Why fight in the name of religion?
Does it make sense to you?

Rebecca Barker (13)
Abington High School

I Will Be With You Again

When the shops sell smiles,
When the rain turns pink,
When the stars are gone from the sky,
I will be with you again,
When the trees sink into the ground
And the sea is dry,
When the world is flat,
I will be with you again,
When the words are gone
And the love is dead,
When the sparkle leaves your eye,
I will be with you again.

Natalie Hackett (14)
Abington High School

Shopping Trip

I enter the shop and grab a trolley,
With not much time to spare,
I whizz in through the double doors,
And fly past customer care.

Zooming straight down the aisles,
Past spices and savoury cakes,
Then over to the meat counter,
To buy two half-pound steak.

Then I dash to the freezer section,
And pick up some frozen peas,
I hurry to the delicatessen,
And grab some Leicester cheese.

Finally on to the tills,
I'll pay with credit card,
Queuing takes fifteen minutes,
Damn, but shopping is hard!

With all my stuff in bags,
I struggle out to the car,
This week's shopping is over,
And I think to myself, *hurrah!*

James Tipler (13)
Abington High School

Small Animal Limerick

I've got a guinea pig called Speedy,
He runs very fast indeedy,
I wanted a cat,
Mum said, 'No!' to that,
Maybe I'll have a parrot called Seedy!

Louise Griggs (14)
Abington High School

Suffering In Pain

The pain I feel from all the things
I've been through
Makes me sick to tell you
I can't believe the life I had
The suffering goes straight to my head.

The things I've been through are not a laughing matter
To see my friend suffering was not a lot of laughter
Because she was one of the best
Better than the rest.

Although I'm only 13, I've seen so much grief
Nobody could ever believe
I wish I could wake up and it would be just a dream
But this is not how life seems
Hopefully, happiness will come my way
Into my dreams and take me away.

Harpreet Sehmi (13)
Abington High School

Autumn Time

Ravishing autumn rich and sharp,
Terracotta leaves falling down,
Birds fly away to a hotter place on Earth,
While the swaying of the wind falls down on us all.

The trees are getting barer,
The days are getting darker,
The mist and fog are appearing,
The burning fire of the sun is over now,
So autumn is here at last!

Tejal Solanki (13)
Abington High School

The Virus

You cannot hear me, you cannot touch me, you cannot taste me,
Yet I live deep within you and affect your very being and anatomy.

I am the silent assassin, the dark undertaker, the uninvited guest,
I can infect any part of your body or your mind or even your chest.

You try to stop me and kill me with your medical technology,
But I mutate, replicate and simulate with my personal biology.

I am just a single cell and yet I spread great fear throughout your race,
And I have destroyed whole civilisations, both here and in space.

For eons you have dreaded me from Adam and Eve, to you of today,
I have played your lived, your children and just will not go away.

Having now wreaked havoc and become master of all that is man,
You have introduced me to a new target made of silicone in a can.

Yes, I can now attack and infest man's new friend, namely
                                        the computer,
I erase memories, crash networks, plant Trojans, the electronic looter.

Now master of flesh and lord of the virtual reality,
Your only hope is to re-find your spirituality.

Sam Moffoot (13)
Abington High School

Wind Crawling

The wind crawls through the night,
Wrapping its arms around everything it meets,
Touching people with its ice-cold fingertips,
Turning every droplet of water into ice with its chilly blow,
Twirling between houses and trees
Off into the darkness.

Natalie Spurden (13)
Abington High School

The Beast Next Door

Like a hunter, it hunts
And stays by my side,
It stops, it waits,
Until it is time.

With a hunched back
And sharp claws,
It is close,
It has been here before.

It sits here, every day,
For an hour.
It has foul yellow eyes,
That force me to cower.

It sits with me,
I try to hide,
In my English lesson,
She sits by my side.

Joe Ladlow (13)
Abington High School

My Friend

My good friend is always there,
He's sweet, helpful and really cares.

We share our emotions, secrets as well,
He's one of the best mates and I'm not ashamed to tell.

When we're together there's a connection very strong,
But when we're apart particularly wrong.

I love him so much, I can never compare,
My friendship with him, something I'd never share.

Samantha Houlihan (13)
Abington High School

The Waiting Room

I am waiting in the waiting room
For my new nose,
I hope everyone approves
Of the one that I have chose.

I am waiting in the waiting room,
For my new eyes,
I will no longer walk the streets
Wearing a disguise.

I am waiting in the waiting room
For my new ears,
The ones that I already have
Bring everyone to tears.

I am waiting in the waiting room
For my new chin,
They are going to reshape it
And hold it with a pin,

So after some time I returned
To my humble abode, my home,
My mother didn't recognise me
And threw a dangerous stone.

It destroyed my new and plastic face,
A sight most disturbing to see,
I sat down and thought, *what is the point*?
And said, 'It is good to be me!'

Jake Wright (14)
Abington High School

The Flaming Hunter

It quietly lays dormant,
Its sleeping just begun,
The beauty it displays,
And the damage already done.

The outside draped in a layer
A calm layer of peace,
Yet inside it is twisted,
A cruelty never to cease.

It is a volcano,
With a tiger's heart,
A heart of pure cruelty,
That's not played its part.

While the tiger prepares to attack,
The volcano bubbles inside,
They both strike their prey,
With a tiger's pride.

The tiger pounces,
And boils its foe,
Their strength bound,
By the fury of woe.

While sleeping both are beautiful,
Yet danger lurks nearby,
For you must not disturb them,
Or else expect to die . . .

Adam Gibbins (13)
Abington High School

I'll Stop!

I'll stop thinking of you when . . .
Milk is pink
And we get orange money,
When grass is yellow
And Pooh Bear stops loving honey,
When fishes can't swim
And our blazers aren't black.
When Mary hasn't got a lamb
And when it's Jill and Jack.
I'll stop dreaming of you when . .
Dinosaurs are back
And I sneeze out my ears,
When snow isn't cold
And I cry purple tears,
When we live in space
And the bike has square wheels,
When the sun shines at night
And Ainsley stops cooking meals.
I'll stop loving you . . .
When my eyes change colour
And apples are blue,
When the sea runs dry
And cats go moo,
When Christmas is in March
And water runs green,
When teabags make coffee
And Santa has been seen.

Danni Palmer (13)
Abington High School

Go To Bed To Wake Up

Go to bed to wake up
Turn off the tap for water to come out
Cover your ears to stop the smell
Go to bed to wake up
Stand up to sit down
Applaud a failure
And praise a fool

Go to bed to wake up
Plant a tree to grow a seed
Open a window to keep in the heat
Go to bed to wake up
Oxfam help the rich
Healthy dogs get put down
And you score to lose

Go to bed to wake up
Rubbers reveal pictures
Parrots are taught to be silent
Go to bed to wake up
Give to gain
Whisper to be heard
Thank your enemy tonight . . .

And go to bed to sleep.

Tom Green (13)
Abington High School

Nature

Nature has many faces
All in different forms
From the soft swaying of a simple tree
To a rabbit, bear or you and me

In the moonlit sky
The wolf will howl
As new life begins
When a horse gives birth to its foal

If you look up
You will see the sun sitting in the sky
You can also see the eagle
Flying so very high

In the sea the fish will swim
As the seals lie on the bay
And the sly and ferocious shark
Attacks the unsuspecting prey

The mountain tops so high
Covered in a white sheet of snow
There lives the sure-footed mountain goat
It's where the streams start to flow

But all this is coming to an end
With the industry of man
Animals are supposed to survive
There are very few who can

They dump the toxic waste
Into the once pearl-blue sea
If they want a bit of paper
They must cut down a beautiful tree

Their ways they must try to end
Or it will, come to an end.

Craig Appleby (13)
Abington High School

I'd Be Standing

When the shops sell smiles
And the rain is pink
Turn the tap on
And milk the sink.
I'd be standing here waiting.
When the sea is dry
And land is wet
When words are gone
With the sunset
I'd be standing here waiting.
When hearts are evil
And love is dead
Pillows are rock
And as tough as old bread
I'd be standing here waiting.

Kirstie Abbott (13)
Abington High School

Daintily

The little girl sat on her grandmother's knee and asked
'What does daintily mean?'

The grandmother replied,
'Daintily is a little girl dancing,
Daintily is a purring kitten,
Dainty is a seedling growing,
Daintily are a baby's fingers and toes,
Daintily is a field mouse,
Daintily making its home,
Daintily are the crops that wave in the wind,
Daintily is a bird making its nest.'

When the loving old woman looked down she saw a little girl
Sleeping daintily on her lap.

Alice Hale (11)
Loughborough High School

Searching

I'm searching for a place where I fit in,
For a place where my views are not thrown in the bin.

I'm searching for a place where I'm treated like everyone else
                                              and more,
I'm searching for a place not like before,
I'm searching for a place because my feelings are hurt and sore,
I'm searching for a place because I don't belong anymore.

I'm searching for a place because things are not the same,
I'm searching for a place because I have a lot of shame.

I'm searching for a place where someone knows my name,
It's not like I'm asking for fame.

I'm searching for a place far far away,
I'm searching for a place because I don't want to stay.
I'm searching for a place because I can't deny, my life is becoming
                                                a big lie.
I'm being bullied and you will never know what it's like,
When they push you against the wall ready for a fight.

Vaila Ormiston (11)
Loughborough High School

Brightly . . .

Brightly the television flickers in the night,
Brightly shines the cascading moonlight,
Brightly cats' eyes sparkle in the dark,
Brightly the lamp post flickers in the park,
Brightly the sun beams, even on a cloudy day,
Brightly a child's smile sparkles in an affectionate way,
Brightly flickers hope in a sea of despair,
Brightly beams tiredness from wear and tear,
But brightest of all shines love and affection,
Where ignorance and nastiness takes a deflection,
If there's no love on the outside, there will be deep down,
Because everyone, in our eyes, wears a crown.

Elise Cole (11)
Loughborough High School

The Good Old-Fashioned Apple

It's boring being an apple,
Sitting on the sill
Watching people come and go,
Doing what they will.

I've watched the pears
Seen them go
And see the orange flee
And now I'm just wondering
What's to become of me?

It's not fair!
I just don't get it,
Am I less juicy
Than a tiny pear?

But then this next bit,
I really cannot bear
Was I sent here from the orchards
Just to sit and stare?

But really what did happen,
To the good old-fashioned apple?

Victoria Smith (12)
Loughborough High School

Quickly

Quickly the rocket shoots up to space,
Quickly the car goes mad to race,
Quickly the cheetah races its meat,
Quickly Paula races to compete,
Quickly the strong lightning strikes,
Quickly the judges choose their likes.

Siobhan Sullivan (12)
Loughborough High School

The Cellar Girl

My life is a gloom,
In this cellar of misery,
I want a proper life,
Out of these cellar doors.

All I have are these rags,
My master has a whip and wouldn't care for anyone.
I sleep and eat on this cold floor
And all I eat is this bread, raw.

I sweep the floors day and night
And must do everything perfect and right,
No colour in my life, no matter how hard I try,
Dark shadows lay drifting over my face.

In my world flowers are black,
Brooms are all I have in my sack
And every day I dream of when
I will loved and be cared for.

I have no family to hug me
Or tell me how wonderful I am.
I just lay here in this dark room
And stare at the webbed ceiling.

Shreenal Ghelani (11)
Loughborough High School

The Rain And The Sun

The pitter-patter of the rain is coming through the door
All you can hear is it coming more and more
All you can really do is look at the floor
And it is a real bore

So I look up and out comes the sun
So I go out to have some fun
Then I call all my friends and tell them to come
Then we all play about and run.

Anika Karia (11)
Loughborough High School

Outside

Outside is . . .

The one place you can breathe fresh air,
The place where parents give much care.
The place where you can feel the ground,
The place where children run around.

Outside is . .

The place where the birds sing from the trees,
The place where children scrape their knees.
The place where you can smell fresh grass,
The place where minutes and hours pass.

Outside is . . .

The place where children build their dens,
The place where you hang out with friends.
The place where the sun's in the sky,
The place where butterflies fly by.

Outside is . . .

The place where you can ride your bike,
The place where people go on hikes.
The place where you can scream and shout,
The place where you can mess about.

Lucy Hagger (11)
Loughborough High School

The Dragon's Tale

Down in the depths of the shadowy gloom
Lives a fire-breathing monster guarding its gold
Scaly and fearsome, mind only to kill
Haunting the lives of young and old

From mouth to mouth, rumours are spreading
This perilous monster is nearing our town
Heroic young knights in shining armour
Gather to slay it from miles around

The foremost adventurer departs with pride
Mounting his sleek and gallant steed
Preparing to defeat this bloodythirsty demon
No doubt many others will follow his lead

Entering the dark and murky forest
His eyes strain sharply through the cloak of gloom
Pushing his weary mount ever onwards
Second by second nearing their doom

Approaching the foreboding fiery mountain
Heart in his mouth he bravely dismounts
Unsteadily stumbling shakily forward
Entering the cave, the profound fear mounts

Suddenly the dragon in all its fury
Steps with menace out from the dark
Towering above his tiny opponent
For the murderous dragon, this is merely a lark

Quickly the knight lunges forward
Sword cutting swiftly through the air
Pierced through the heart, his lifeblood streaming
The dragon lies dead on the floor of his lair.

Hannah Andrews (12)
Loughborough High School

A Big Mistake

She'd read the stories,
She'd learnt at school,
Why did she go and break the rule?

The little girl,
Who's in her teens
Went on and changed society.

On Internet
In some chat room,
Is where she met Mr Lagoom.

The blasted man
Who's in his forties,
Told her he was in his twenties!

That girl believed
What this man said!
He even said his name was Ed!

These were all lies,
She didn't know
And so said, 'I'll see you tomorrow!'

They met for lunch,
In the café O' Par,
But when she got there she was shoved in his car!

She has now been missing
For 83 days,
So please, please don't make her mistake.

Emma Haig (12)
Loughborough High School

I Wonder As I Wander

I wonder as I wander
Beneath the morning sky
Why do all the people
Just come . . and then they die?

I wonder as I wander
Along the dewy grass
Why are some people so sensitive
And some just let it pass?

I wonder as I wander
As morning turns to night
How can we be reassured
That everything's alright?

I wonder as I wander
While climbing up the stairs
Why do some animals eat us
Like sharks or grizzly bears?

I wonder as I wander
As I slip into my bed
Why doesn't God just destroy us all
And make something new instead?

Katie Gray (12)
Loughborough High School

The Person Of Mystery

This person is small and unnoticed,
Kind and protective,
Tidy and unselective,
Gentle and careful,
Friendly and cheerful,
Helpful and caring,
Loving and sharing,
Who is she?

She is what we all could be.

Laura Mason (11)
Loughborough High School

Growing Up

Every day meant something new,
Exploring the tangly tree at the end of the garden,
The excitement of waking to a birthday bouncy castle,
Just below my bedroom window.
The disappointment of asking a visiting Santa for a puppy
And receiving a jigsaw.
It wasn't long before things began to change.
Somehow everything became harder.
I was desperate to play in the garden,
I wanted to escape, to create another world for myself.
Now I wake every day and I feel I know what's going to happen.
Growing up can be hard,
But I still feel excited when I go to bed on Christmas Eve.

Betsy Chadbourn (11)
Loughborough High School

Life

Slowly the petals break off the flower head and drift away,
Slowly the frost covers the ground threatening anything in its path,
Slowly the leaves fall from the trees' tired branches.

Slowly lives are lost,
Slowly hearts are broken,
Slowly tears fall from faces,
Slowly everything deteriorates.

Leaving nothing but blank
Desperation fills happy, joyful hearts.

This is what people go through and what life becomes,
So look after and enjoy life with loved ones.

Charlotte O'Connor (11)
Loughborough High School

If . . .

If chocolate was eaten with every meal
And no one had heard of sprouts!
If pigs woofed and dogs squealed
And cats were fat and stout!

If roundabouts went the other way
And Englishmen drove on the right!
If law was created, and no one could obey
And day was dark with moonlight!

If oranges were green and bananas were blue
And nothing on Earth was yellow!
If tables didn't exist, like two times two
And a whisper was known as a bellow.

If you got told off for not talking in class
And handing in homework on time!
If exams were there not to pass
And poems could never rhyme!

If . . .
If . . .
If . . .
If only!

Bernadette Ellerby (11)
Loughborough High School

The Dark

The light switches off, but my fear switches on,
The dark surrounds me.
I curl up under my quilt,
But that won't help me.
I'm enveloped in thick, black darkness,
It smothers me.
I reach for my teddy bear, but can't find it,
I'm alone.
I tell myself, 'Go to sleep,'
But I'm wide awake.
The dark swirls and dances,
I'm lost.
Strange things leer at me,
But I can't see them.
The dark makes me blind to everything,
What is there?
The inky-black void is threatening,
I'm trapped.
I tremble with fright in my prison of fear,
Rescue me.
I can't escape.

Rosie Stafford (11)
Loughborough High School

A Ballet Dancer

A ballet dancer is full of grace,
With her arms she does embrace
The stage on which she spreads some joy,
Moving around like a clockwork toy.
Like a swan floating over the stage,
To the musical notes being played.
Moving like a delicate butterfly,
Watch her spin and leap way up high.

See the curves of her hips
And the pink on her lips,
Dancing with precision and care
And neatly pinned hair.
As she jumps she looks agile,
When she lands she looks fragile.
Moving her limbs and torso,
Enveloped in a tutu and bow.

Her routine unfolds before
Your eyes,
The routine she has rehearsed
A hundred times.
The stage lights burn on her
Glowing face,
Glistening down to her shoes
Tied with lace.

She looks out to the crowd,
As the audience cheer her
She begins to look proud,
At the fact that she can entertain
And her wonderful talents
Have brought her fame!

Amanda Dalby (13)
Loughborough High School

The Lonely Man

Silhouetted against a red canvas
Watching a glowing ball setting into the sea
The lonely man sits silently thinking
Thinking of happy memories.

At first glance you'd think him stern
And his eyes aren't exactly forget-me-not blue
But if you'd look deeper than his tired face
You'd find that this man is a person too.

He comes to the beach in the evening quite often
To the spot where his wife and children came
He hears them whispering from the sea
'Come join us Dad, come join the game.'

The waves tumble tormenting and fierce
His wife's spirit echoes in his mind
The lonely man rises to his feet
He takes off his hat and leaves it behind.

The waves are like horses and gallop towards him
They pounce like a cat that's caught its prey
One last gulp and life is sucked from him
As the strong current sweeps him away.

No one noticed the lonely man was gone
The wind had swept his hat away
But there were strange footprints leading up to the sea
And a dent in the sand where the lonely man once lay.

Naomi Pakenham (13)
Loughborough High School

The Horse

The horse is a majestic creature,
With a mane and tail as fine as silk,
Its every move is so very graceful,
As it races through the cold night air.

As it gallops, its hooves hardly touch the ground,
Its legs are powerful as any engine,
A mysterious, ghostly shadow,
As it races through the cold night air.

Its nostrils flare as it whinnies,
Its tail streams behind like a silken banner,
But it never slows down,
As it races through the cold night air.

As it races from danger,
Its hooves pound like the ocean on a windy day,
Foam streams from its mouth like ocean spray,
As it races through the cold night air.

It never stumbles,
Or loses its strength,
It never looks back,
As it races through the cold night air.

Nicole Turner (14)
Loughborough High School

The Boy On The Beach

As the sun was falling in the sky,
Relaxing the atmosphere over the Thai coast.
The sea slowly rippling over the sand,
Dampening down this beautiful land.

A young boy played along the coast,
Taking life in his stride, without a care in the world.
With his toy horse he played on his own,
With his toy horse he played alone.

On the horizon islands you see,
Dark silhouettes in the distance break up the sea.
In front of these there was a quaint boat,
Which was bobbing, gently afloat.

The boy on the coast threw a stick,
Into the sea, for his dog to go and fetch for him.
Out he scrambled, shaking himself off,
Dancing around then beginning to cough.

The sea had been coming in gradually,
Step by step, moment by moment, swallowing up the shore,
Now the sea was upon the boy on the beach,
His dad said, 'Bed,' and he let out a screech.

Lauren Kluckow (14)
Loughborough High School

My Little Sister

My little sister is really terrible
She's truly bad
She put my hamster in the oven
And snails in my brother's bed, poor lad

She jumped on the radio
She kicked me in the shin
She pushed my mum in the pond
She stabbed my dad with a pin

She dug up worms in the garden
And put them on a plate
They made me sick
You know the ones you really hate

She's always poking the cat
She's always kissing the dog
She's always stealing Mum's best hat
She looks like a warthog

She hits me on the head
She pokes me in the eye
She calls me names
I've no idea why

She can be good at times
I love my sister really
It wouldn't be the same without her
I love my sister dearly.

Francesca Smith (12)
Loughborough High School

Never Worth Forgetting

Her hands alone told a story,
Each crease like a permanent memory.

Her face, wrinkled like tissue paper,
Which highlighted her expression.

She looked exhausted and worn,
She had worked hard for as long as
Her mind could remember.

A big family she belonged to,
But outgrown them all.

She sat and thought,
She sat and thought.

Those memories she keeps
Are never worth forgetting.

Loved by hundreds,
Adored by thousands and
A friend to many more.

This woman, her memories and all,
Will be remembered,
For she alone is never worth forgetting.

Emily Wainwright (13)
Loughborough High School

The Golden Temple

In the heart of India,
A place called Amritsar,
Lies a temple where the Sikhs worship.
It's a building of gold,
Surrounded by water
Which has been made holy by the Sikh gods.
The sun beams down upon the holy shrine
Making the gold glisten and shine.
Everyone must walk upon the marble floors
Which are as hot as an iron.
The site of the temple brings tears of joy,
As the view is incomparable
To anything else in the world.
The holy water surrounding the temple,
Sways in the warm breeze
And twinkles in the presence of the gold.
The Sikhs bathe in the water
As it is believed
To rid them of all their sins.
You leave the water free of all bad.
You enter a new world
And are sure to be glad.
The holy scriptures
Lie in their place after 300 years
With not a mark on it, no tear to be seen.
It contains all the Sikh knowledge
For those that are keen.
As night arrives, the lights are turned on,
To reflect the whole image
To the water.
The site is made even more picturesque,
Simply blinding to the eye.

Simran Chaggar (13)
Loughborough High School

Treasured Memories

Encased in a strong father's arms,
A young child can come to no harm.
Sparks of happiness floating throughout the air,
Without any bad thoughts, worries or cares.

Happy as if upon cloud nine,
There must be an end to this happy time.
So down comes the force of a lethal sharp knife
And ends the enjoyment of the father's life.

The child now sits alone and cold,
Abandoned and lost at 10 years old.
They're left wondering how, when and why?
As their little hearts break, they slowly begin to cry.

Down their velvet cheeks stroll tears of glass,
A pale, devastated look on their face is cast.
They peer at the stars that are gleaming bright,
Transfixed on the brightest against the black winter's night.

Christmas is near, just around the corner,
But no joy is destined for this young little mourner.
As they lay their dear beloved to rest,
They think of the times that were the best.

Birthdays, Christmases, days of pure fun,
Days when the children were still so young.
Playing in the garden with a bat and ball,
Back when the child was naïve and small.

Although it has taken a very long while,
The child now wears a shimmering smile.
Memories now remembered of times that were fun, crazy and mad,
But what is treasured most, the memory of their dad.

Fiona Clegg (14)
Loughborough High School

Oh Those Were The Days

She sits out on the veranda in her rocking chair,
Daydreaming of her younger years,
That room that was so full of life and cheers,
Oh those were the days.

How many times she would stand and stare,
At that garden, now so cold and bare,
She had met her true love there,
Before his life was snatched away.

On the swing he used to push her, flowers in her hair,
Oh what times they had together, oh what memories to share,
But all cannot stay happy, as that is never true,
Cos war is such a monstrous thing and survivors are only few.

Her withered hands caress the dress she used to wear,
Sadly now extremely threadbare,
Memories flood back, belle of the ball she used to be, living
Without a care,
She broke many a young man's heart, they begged fo r a dance,
But never did she find romance,
Like the true love she once possessed.

Never will she cease searching for that one true love,
Who protects her from up above,
But sooner than she thinks, they will embrace again, never to let go,
In God's paradise dream world.

A bittersweet ending to this love story,
As God works in mysterious ways,
For this lady, now so old and frail,
Is reliving those very happy days.

Rebecca Williams (13)
Loughborough High School

My Life

Hundreds of years ago it seems,
I fulfilled all my hopes and dreams.
In some heavenly place was I,
I had everything that I desired.

A happy family, a husband I loved,
Sweet little children, every day we hugged.
We laid down, watched the stars together,
Sometimes it seemed we'd lain there forever.

We walked together, holding hands,
All bare-footed upon the sand.
Every day seemed such bliss,
The children's laughter, which now I miss.

On a cold and stormy day,
Was the last I saw of my family.
They all hugged me before going to school
And then they drove away.

When I heard the terrible news,
I couldn't bear to listen,
I had lost everything in my life,
All my happiness and how much I miss them.

Now I am just a wrinkly old woman,
Not really capable of much.
People come and make me cups of tea,
But no one really cares much about me.

Seneka Nakagawa (14)
Loughborough High School

Alone?

Inactive on the secluded golden carpet,
Passively watching the world go by,
Watching nature tend to their young,
Watching the crisp white clouds
Gently fuse together wrapping up the sun's glow,
Watching his past relive again

As he has waded through the years,
Seeing many a sunset, with many a people,
Does anybody still recognise his charm?
Is anybody still aware of his glorifying presence
That he would anticipate all those sunsets ago?
Is anybody replying to the love that he has to offer?

The white horse opens up to the golden carpet,
Munching on stories and hearsay,
Every bite, reliving a memory,
Every bite, welling up emotions
As if it has taken place an instant ago,
Every bite, washing a part of his heart away.

Philippa Aspinall (13)
Loughborough High School

Shopping Ingredients

First of all drop your ingredients into the bank,
Place collected money mixture into small purse,
Switch on car to 60 mph and pile in decorative young ladies.
Turn off car and leave to cool in multi-storey car park
And bubble into Burberry.
Leave Burberry to cool and move into Gucci!
Stay in Gucci for half an hour then leave and simmer into Prada.
Leave all shops, go back to multi-storey,
Turn on car and move back home!

Helena Dean (12)
Loughborough High School

So Little Time

Here I am alone and cold,
No one here, no hand to hold.
It's got to end, I know it will,
But yet I can remember still,
When I was just a little lad
I played in these waves, what fun I had!
Where has the time gone? I need to know,
I want to stay, don't let me go!
We all come down here every year
And every time I end up here.
Sitting down beside the sea,
What shall I do? Old lonely me!
The fisherman pulls in his line,
I realise there's not much time.
We've got to go home now, it's always the same.
The holiday's over, what a shame!

Louisa Ackerley (13)
Loughborough High School

Daily Shopping Recipe

First of all drop your ingredients into the bank.
Place collected money mixture into purse.
Switch on car to 180 miles per hour.
Pile in decorative young ladies.
Turn off car and leave to cool in the car park.
Hurry to get your friends into the shops.
Start preparing the clothes that you are going to try on.
Then once they are prepared pour into bags.
Then before transferring into car leave for two hours.
Then, when in car, wait for half an hour
Then check everything is hot before tipping into house.
Then again allow to cool
In bed at 11pm.

Sophie Heffernan (12)
Loughborough High School

Early Morning Lesson!

Lessons start early in the morning
Everyone sits there tired and yawning
We listen to a teacher droning on
Waiting for the bell to ring like a gong
Every so often we check the clock
Itch our heads and pull up our socks
We look down at the work in front
Oh no! My pencil is blunt!
I get up and go to the bin
Sharpen my pencil and pick up a drawing pin
Glance at the clock on the wall
Five minutes, then I can leave and head for the lunch hall
The teacher finishes speaking
Oh no! My pen's leaking!
Two minutes left then I can leave
My friend opposite gives a great heave
One minute, I really can't wait
This lesson better not finish late
50 seconds of torture left
Someone yawns, she is sitting on my left
30 little seconds then I'm free
Oh no! After lunch we have double PE
20, 10, I'm counting down in my head
The clock hand is turning as though it's made of lead
5, 4, I stare at the windowpane
3, oh dear it seems to be rain
Two, ring-a-ding dong, ring-a-ding
Yes! Out of lessons one second early
I pass a girl in my form looking rather surly
Out the door now I'm free
Free till double PE!

Rachael Beasley (13)
Loughborough High School

Where Would You Live?

How would you like to fly
Get away from it all?
How would you like to break away
Leave all stresses behind?
How would you like to stop
Make your life stand still?
How would you like to rest
Sleep the days away?

How would you like to dwell
In a world of peace and love?
How would you like to live
In a world with no war?
How would you like to be
Safe from all conflict?
How would you like to live
In my beautiful world?

I would love to fly,
Get away from it all.
I would love to break away,
Leave everything behind.
I would love to stop,
Stop all pain and hurt.
I would love to live
In this world of peace.
Can't we all share this dream?

Becky Jackson (12)
Loughborough High School

Heaven

In our afterlife, where do we go?
Is there a Heaven? How do we know?
When we arrive at those pearly white gates,
What will happen, what becomes our fate?
Before we can enter that heavenly place,
There is one question that we must face.
A question so important, the answer we give
Will allow us the chance to once again live.
A chance to remember a moment that's past
A special memory that will always last.
Our fondest memory that we can remember,
That hot summer's day, that snowy December,
That one happy memory of family and friends,
That one favourite memory we hope never ends.
So you give your answer and you are let through
And that one simple memory becomes Heaven for you.

Jaspreet Assi (12)
Loughborough High School

The Show . . .

The grass was green
And the ponies were snorting
The fences were huge
And the judges were sorting
The bell started ringing
To tell me to start
As I came to the fence
Thump! went my heart
I finished the course
And the crowd were chatting
I stopped my pony
And gave him lots of patting
Down came the sun
Up came the moon
What a great afternoon.

Charlotte Agar (12)
Loughborough High School

Olympia Jumping

Into the arena,
The show starts at last,
The crowds are all screaming,
The horses are fast.

The audience go silent,
As the jumping begins,
The jumps are very high,
With brightly coloured wings.

The jumping has ended,
The jump off yet to start,
The horses are excited
And they're ready to dart.

After the jump off,
The winner must part,
From the horses out back
And receive their prize at top of the chart.

Katie-Rose Gilmore (12)
Loughborough High School

In The Playground

In the playground I am a horse that runs like the wind.
In the playground I am a dragon that breathes smoke and fire.
In the playground I am a knight of the Round Table
Who fights monsters and rescues damsels in distress.
In the playground I am a mermaid with a long, green, scaly tail.
In the playground I am a bug-eyed troll.
In the playground I am a wizard casting spells.
In the playground I am a bird that soars high in the sky.
In the playground I am a dog chasing cats.
In the playground I am a cat chasing mice.
In the playground I am a mouse eating cheese.
In the playground I can be anything imaginable.
Then the bell rings and I am plain, boring me again,
Trudging in for registration.

Hannah Taylor (12)
Loughborough High School

The Airport

Take a number of people
And mix in with double the amount of luggage,
Leave aside people.
Pour luggage into ready waiting aircraft,
Stir up atmosphere
Until tensions are high.
Add in a considerable amount of rush
And pour in some last minute nerves.
Toss onto plane a few excited children
And pile in frustrated adults.
At this point add in smiling air hostesses
To make the mixture sweeter
And make adults bitter.
Add pilot to bind British Airways together.
Heat up until take-off,
Watch as the tensions rise
And prepare garnish of hopes.
When landed leave for two weeks to cool down.
After they have had time to set,
Repeat the recipe all over again.

Georgina Kearney-Bambridge (12)
Loughborough High School

The Box Room

A box room of things. Many memories,
Grasp attention. Touching times took place there,
A faint memory is just left for me,
A sewing of roses - happy photos,
Why can't they be there? It's Grandma's front room,
'Gazza' a game shoved under the sofa,
A safety glow surrounds me when I'm there.
My place to escape and hide isn't there.
The little box room of memories. Gone!

Meena Mistry (12)
Loughborough High School

The Faces In The Crowd

A face in a crowd unseen,
Merged into the backdrop of life,
Has no name or distinction,
They are just a no one to you.
They do not have hopes or dreams,
Just another face in the crowd.

      But, every face has a name,
      A purpose, an identity,
      They are someone, with feelings,
      They can love, hope, dream, just like you,
      But as they hurry on by,
      To them *you're* the face in the crowd.

So, when next you're in a crowd
And you see an anybody,
Smile; tell them they're somebody,
They do have an identity,
Shout it loud, ask anyone,
Who are the faces in the crowd?

Laura Baker (12)
Loughborough High School

Autumn

Leaves fall to the ground,
They don't make a sound.
The wind swishes and howls.
Shivering are the little barn owls.
There is dew on the grass,
I wonder how long that will last.
I put on my hat, coat and scarf,
In the distance I can hear children laugh.
Soon it will be Bonfire Night,
Which will be a pretty sight.
People turn on the central heating,
It's so cosy, now people are sleeping.

Sophie Wheeler (12)
Loughborough High School

Boyfriend

I appear at the school gate,
Everybody staring,
Why did Gary have to do it yesterday?
Why not dump me tomorrow?
I dash through the corridor,
Up the staircase,
Round the hallways,
Up to the balcony,
Out of the fire exits,
Past the ICT rooms
And into the classroom.
I try to bury my head into my scarf,
But everybody recognises me,
My rosy face turns to an alerting scarlet
And Gary stares at me,
With eyes of stone.
The first lesson is geography,
I enter room 2L and Mr Lashder glares
At everyone, and then suddenly at me,
Why me? What did I ever do to deserve the glare?
It was as if time was on slow down,
I watched Mr Lashder's lips open,
His wonky teeth watching me
And then he speaks . . .
'Nice blusher Elizabeth,
No wonder Gary dumped you!'
Mr Lashder knows,
Death to Gary!

Sarah Grove (12)
Loughborough High School

Masked Girl

Her pastel face,
Ghostly white,
Sleepless eyes,
Hair dark as night.
Eyes are sombre,
Grey and brown,
Lips turned downwards,
Into a frown.
Wispy strands,
Fall onto her face,
A miserable member,
Of the human race.
Inside she's screaming.
But does anyone care?
Do they see her pain?
Do they stop and stare?
No voice to hear,
No words to say,
Her hands are clasped,
Her nails are grey.
Does nobody know her?
Do they dare to ask?
Will she remain the girl,
Hidden by a mask?

Saanchi Sama (13)
Loughborough High School

The Sea

The breakers crash against the chalk-white cliffs.
Pieces of driftwood are captured in the arms of the waves.
Spray leaps up into the air like dolphins.
Miserable, grey clouds spread like a blanket across the sombre sea.
Thunder roars like an angry lion
Bright flashes of lightning pierce the night sky.

Slowly the waves calm down, the thunder rumbles to a silence and the clouds drift away.
Dawn is approaching.
The calm glinting waves begin to lap against the chalk-white cliffs, making no sound at all.
Slimy seaweed and pieces of driftwood are gently carried back to the golden shore.
Fishing boats bob up and down, the sea splashing against their shiny wooden sides.
Seals bask on the endless beach of silk.
Dolphins leap into the air before landing in the sparkling water sending a calm ripple towards the shore.
Letters from faraway places are washed up onto the silky sand in glass bottles.
The sea endlessly drifts towards the rising sun.

Hannah Raban (12)
Loughborough High School

Yellow

Yellow is purple,
Purple is the sun,
For all it doesn't really matter
When our time is done.

All that makes yellow, yellow,
Is the particles in our eyes,
So for all we know,
Purple could be lies.

Gabby MacSweeney (11)
Loughborough High School

The Concert

Gather together all you need
Then join the line up the street
Wrap with relevant scarves and T-shirt
Pour into concert hall

12 tickets a row
That's the most you can have
Compact and bored they rise into the Mexican wave
Start rolling the drums, stirring up the atmosphere

1,500 fans, hot, steaming and waving
Five band members strumming and drumming
Only five minutes to go, why haven't they done this or that?
That's not what the book said would happen

Take them out and cool them down
Start the tidying up,
Then leave the rest for them to do
Maybe serve with baggy clothes or wacky hairstyles.

Sally Smith (12)
Loughborough High School

Colour

Colourfully the rainbow shone throughout the land,
Colourfully the children skipped hand in hand.
Colourfully the birds and bees danced through the air,
Colourfully the land warmed to the sun's glare.

Colourfully the ocean creatures made their way,
Colourfully the tide ebbed and flowed each day.
Colourfully the people splashed and dived,
Colourfully the land and sea stayed alive.

Toni Ashford (11)
Loughborough High School

Recipe For Shopaholics/Cakes!

Place purses in the back seat of car
And heat the engine to 180mph,
Mix up the flour, money and sugar
Until light and fluffy,
Then place into purses.

When you arrive place mixture in oven,
Then bubble into Burberry,
When golden-brown,
Leave to cool on the car bonnet,
Before decorating
With new, expensive clothes.

Once they are cool,
Place into car and drive home,
Best served with new clothes on and
Sprinkled with body glitter.
If they are still hot,
Place in bed for 10 minutes to cool down.

Robyn Vitols (12)
Loughborough High School

Statue

She stands there still, cold and grey,
Her arms in one position, held
By the cold marble stone,
Her cloak carved out of solid rock,
Her face sad and grey,
Standing there weeping,
For being a statue made of stone.
I look at her and wonder
How she must ache,
Sitting in the same position,
All the centuries she's been there,
Through the snow and rain,
Siege and war.

Pooja J Thakor (12)
Loughborough High School

Broken

An old shoelace, a vase on the floor,
A filed nail, the handle of a door,
All of which are material things
But other things can be broken.

A vow made by husband to wife,
The belief of something for all your life,
The respect of a teacher, in and out of school,
The commands of a master follow the rule.

A family when trouble comes to pass,
Your confidence is like a sheet of glass,
Pride and honour can fall apart,
Dreams are lost before they start.

The secret told between lifelong friends,
A promise once broken, never mends.
The law when you commit a crime,
But this heart of mine will mend given time.

Catherine Hall (13)
Loughborough High School

Brightly

Brightly the frost sparkles at dawn,
Brightly the sun rises every spring morn.
Brightly the trees sway in the fresh spring breeze,
Brightly the flowers grow again after the freeze.
Brightly the lambs start to leap and jump high,
Brightly their tails swing as if waving goodbye.
Brightly the world spins round in a haze,
Then soon all four seasons have gone past in my gaze.

Rebecca Lait (11)
Loughborough High School

Your World?

The world outside is darkening,
And the days are becoming old,
The night wins over the day,
And the freezing beats the cold.

Arnie takes California,
Beckham scores for Madrid,
Ferdinand's under investigation,
And Labour's in a pit.

The Americans are fighting terrorism,
So England joins the fun,
Police are catching all sorts,
The rebels are on the run.

Lifeboats save on the sea,
When the autumn sea is raging,
Ambulances help on land,
When the night-time wind is blowing

The trees outside are reddening,
The leaves are all around,
The flowers are quickly dying,
The apples are falling down.

The house is warm and inviting,
It's very cold outside,
Autumn and winter are meeting,
It's nearly time to hide.

The world outside is changing,
It never stops to watch,
October's nearly over,
We had better change the clocks!

Helen Cartwright (11)
Loughborough High School

Death On The Cherwell

There was a darkness all around me
A sadness and a shame
Which made me curse the benefits
Of infamy and fame
I knew he would come back to me
He promised that he would
And so I went on living
For him, I knew I should
I looked after our small daughter
And as she was nearing four
Her father knocked a couple of times
Upon our wooden door
It felt like he'd been gone forever
Though he'd wandered for barely a year
I realised with a smile that
I was glad that he was here
But a fateful day in the Cherwell
He took his very last breath
He tripped and fell in the water
And slowly sank down to his death
Our daughter was all alone then
I couldn't live without him
I watched as his body descended
His chances of living were slim
I closed my eyes and I followed
I never was very brave
I'd have died without him anyway
So we both had a watery grave.

Sophy Nash (14)
Loughborough High School

The Other Side

In the centre of the town,
There is a face among the crowd.
Watching people passing by,
A look of longing in his eyes.

They walk past in designer shoes,
A different pair for every mood.
He sits and holds his lucky cap,
A tartan rug across his lap.

He counts up what he's made today,
A little more than yesterday.
Enough to get him food to eat,
Plus some spare for an extra treat.

It's just loose change to you and me,
We give it away so easily.
I only wish that you could know,
Just how far a pound can go.

When darkness falls, he wraps up tight,
Fights the cold till morning light.
He takes a little time to pray
And thanks the Lord for another day.

Catherine Sowerbutts (14)
Loughborough High School

The Lonely Scarecrow

Standing, waiting, in a field of corn,
Through the night, until the morn,
Idly watching crows all day,
Whilst farmers reap and sow the hay.

Two broomsticks to serve as bones
And clothes to wear from various homes,
His spindly fingers stuffed with hay,
Blow in the wind and scare birds away.

His button eyes glow with joy,
At the sight of a girl or a boy.
Perhaps they will come and climb over the stile,
Into the field and make him smile.

A hole in his hat and the ground at his feet,
He suffers from coldness and from the heat.
His hair made of hay, shimmers like gold,
But even that has started to mould.

A scarf round his neck and a hole in his heart,
He knows how to do his part.
For his only pleasure throughout the day,
Is to blow in the wind and scare birds away.

Sarah Oatley (15)
Loughborough High School

When Darkness

Morning breaks
Out comes the angel
Goes out to the lake
The ducks quack at the angel
Happy, she is
The holy one, the angel
In eternal bliss
This is, for the angel . . .

The colours, shining
Gold, blue, crimson, gold
Reflected in the lake, never dying
Shining through secrets, never to be told
But soon comes black
The colours go
The bliss cracks
And down comes the angel

Darkness falls
So does the angel
Heaven calls
But there is no angel
Blood is shed
Blood of an angel
No words is said
Again by the angel
Where has she gone?
Our princess, the angel
Why won't she come?
Our princess, the angel
No answer comes from
Our sister the angel
Why does no sound come?
From my sister
My sister
The angel . . .

Sarah Bowden (12)
Loughborough High School

September 11th

How can people do this,
To those innocent lives?
Crash four planes
And kill so many,
Why? Why? Why?

Don't get your own back,
By killing all those friends.
Did you see the people
Trying to save their lives?

People jumping out,
From levels high and low
Don't start World War III,
Please just leave us alone.

I don't understand,
Why?
Why would you
Kill all those lives?

People are innocent,
People are brave,
You've just ruined,
All their lives.

As I said,
Lives are lost,
Don't start a world war,
It'll lose more.

Leave us,
Leave us,
Leave us forever.
Let us get on,
With our everyday life.

Francesca Hicks (11)
Loughborough High School

Memories

Tom O'Myre opened his door,
He was 87 that day,
He put on his dirty, moth-eaten boots,
On the 21st of May.

He thought of his pretty wife, Mary,
As the sun began to rise,
She would have been 83 that day,
If she was still alive.

He thought of the big old oak tree,
That they sat under when she was ill,
He imagined her beautiful, smiling face
And wished she sat there still.

He remembered his pals from when he was young,
It was a shame they'd all passed on,
He remembered how cheeky they'd been,
He was lonely now that they'd gone.

He passed by the front of the corner shop,
He remembered that's where they had played,
Six kids ran out, the owner behind,
Who shouted, 'You haven't yet paid!'

But by now he was tired of the world,
He thought it was just a pest,
So, slowly, he wandered back home again,
To have some tea and a rest.

Tom O'Myre opened his door,
He was 87 that day,
He looked up to the sky, the wind on his face
And his spirit drifted away.

Lorna Sowerbutts (11)
Loughborough High School

Gently

Gently the waves wash over the sand,
Gently a dog is petted by a loving hand,
Gently the wind blows through the trees,
Gently rustling the crisp golden leaves.

Gently the clouds move through the sky,
Gently a bird floats on high,
Gently the wolf sounds its call,
Gently the autumn leaves begin to fall.

Gently a baby stirs in its rest,
Gently a mother feeds chicks in a nest,
Gently the seeds the farmer sows,
Gently a flower begins to grow.

Gently a mother speaks to her child,
Gently an animal creeps in the wild,
Gently and softly grazes the sheep,
Gently someone, somewhere drifts off to sleep.

Emma Schofield (12)
Loughborough High School

Graffiti

Graffiti in the bathroom down by the bath,
Graffiti in chalk sprawled across the path.

Graffiti on the schoolbooks scribbled across the page,
Graffiti on the table done in a rage.

Graffiti on houses from a red spray can,
Graffiti on the windows sprayed by a man.

Graffiti on clothes gives it a funk,
Graffiti on hair like a 60s' punk.

Graffiti you can see could be good,
Parents say you shouldn't but you still think you should.

Jenna Lee & Jenny Turner (12)
Lutterworth High School

Wondering

I sit here and wonder what to do. Where do I go?
What do I do?
I don't understand what is there in life,
A whole big mystery just waiting for me.

I glance at the wipe board, the teacher writes,
It rubs out. Where does it go?
Is there a land beyond the board rubber?
Is there a magical world?
A whole big mystery just waiting for me.

Lying on my bed staring at the ceiling, thinking
And wondering, pondering on this one question,
Where do I go when I'm gone? Is it a magical door that comes?
Is there a Heaven full of angels and a god,
Or is there a Hell full of devils and fire?
Is there another world?
A whole big mystery just waiting for me.

I wonder what to wonder about, I collapse on my bed
And look around at my room,
Is it real, is it life?
Is there another world beyond this place?
Where do I go? What do I do?
I don't understand what is there in life,
Is it a whole big mystery just waiting for me?

Jodie Brightmore (12)
Lutterworth High School

Blood Of The Phoenix

From which a phoenix rises,
A hot embrace of colours,
Protecting, keeping you safe,
Light and love are its gift,
Melted by a snowdrift.
Now it is angry,
Now it reaps revenge,
Wood fuels its anger,
Like a juggernaut it destroys,
Woodlands in its quake,
Water is now too late.
Obsessive in its clutch,
Wind and it now allies,
No longer must it wait,
Crackling with laughter,
Spitting in your face.
It will never conquer with rain in its path,
As it falls the fire hisses with pain,
Now it is all ashes,
The dust that symbolises death,
'I never meant to hurt you,' it calls.
From which a phoenix falls.

Peter Rowe (12)
Lutterworth High School

Water

It can kill with one blow but save lives in seconds
It is powerful, forceful and flowing
It can cause a thousand deaths but save a thousand lives
It can destroy good or evil
It can pour down or not come for years
It can be smooth or rough, gentle or deadly
You can float or sink, live or die
You can live off it or die without it
It can be powerful like a lion after its prey
It can be gentle like a flowering garden
It can burn you or freeze you
It glistens in the moonlight
Shimmers in the dark
Can destroy a million years of work
Can swallow up all life.

Rebecca Amy Simpson (12)
Lutterworth High School

Fire

It takes life ferociously,
But we need it to survive.
Fire has a mind of its own.
With help from his trusted ally the wind,
Which accelerates devastation.

Scalding, scorching and burning,
These are the things that fire causes.
The height of the flames,
Are extravagantly staturetic.
Beware, be warned, stay clear of fire.

Marcus Ikin (12)
Lutterworth High School

Water

She starts as a trickle,
The source of a brook.
She flows down and down
Into the river, lake or sea.
She can be choppy and icy
Lapping over rocks in a stream.
She can be warm and relaxing,
A bath full of bubbles.
She takes up the shape given,
Whatever the depth.
She comes in all different quantities,
Big or small.
She has a mind of her own
Flowing all over.
She's like a boat on the rapids,
Going at any speed, at any time, anywhere.
She splishes and splashes
And roars like the wind.
She seethes over the shingly shore
And is home to many animals.
She is washed in
And played in, too.
She generates electricity,
And light, and heat.
She is used for cooking food
And is drunk, too.
She gives life, takes life,
In her we can swim,
She can be clean and pure.
Or a dirty brown, full of disease and
Awfully dim.

Brittany Holland (12)
Lutterworth High School

Water

It rocks, it roars, hacking at the rocks bit by bit,
The smooth surface may not be what it seems down below,
It falls and crashes at the end of its journey down to the bottom of the fall,
When people go down you never know if they're going to come back up,
It can be rough and take lives or can be calm and not hurt a single soul,
The people don't know what lies beneath, it can be fishes or
Could be ships, but worst of them all could be bones of the dead innocent humans that don't care and go in even if there is a warning,
It is used to drink, used to save lives and used to wash,
It's the greatest thing in the history of the Earth,
It's used to get from one country to another taking people on their vacations,
The life of animals is underneath the surface and remains of things
Lie down under and now it becomes history.
The canoes glide across reaching incredible speeds but if you're not too careful you could lose control and . . .

Oliver Van Allen (12)
Lutterworth High School

Fire

It roars like a lion getting louder and louder as it reaches its target,
The only warning that it's on its way is that tell-tale smell it creates,
It shows no mercy as everything in its path gets eaten,
Innocent wildlife has no chance as it hungers for more,

Rushing through the forest like a racehorse in a gallop,
Creating choking fumes to pollute the atmosphere,
The heat is intense,
It's a natural menace,
Its light flickers like a disco ball through tree branches,
Sparks spitting help it to spread at an uncontrollable pace,
Only water can dampen its enthusiasm and end its life.

Melissa Creese (12)
Lutterworth High School

Fire

The sizzling colours ravishing red,
Outrageous orange, you'll live yellow and cool blue,
On bonfires you see it spitting embers,
Everywhere ready for fireworks to bang, crackle and pop,
The watching of the flame burning people's lives
It keeps you alive,
You heat food with it,
It is bad for your health,
By smoking, puff by puff, killing your lungs each time,
To make it work you need oxygen,
Ignition and fuel,
It gives you warmth to make you feel stronger,
The touch of the burn can scar you for life,
Water and an extinguisher puts it out,
The brightness of the burn makes you squint and can blind.

Melissa Sharpe (12)
Lutterworth High School

H_2O

It's life
It's death
It can take any shape
Animals depend on it
God's greatest gift
Our most precious resource
Falls from the sky
Outnumbers land by far
Comes out of a tap
Smooth as ice
Shiny like glass
Rough like a rampage
As gentle as grace
Conducts electricity
Envied by other planets.

Joe Seymour (12)
Lutterworth High School

Fire

He burns to kill everything in its path.
Spreading across like an F1 car, jumping
From tree to tree like a flying squirrel, sparking
And spitting as it goes. Hissing to warn the
Creatures to run, jump, fly, elsewhere while
Their home is being demolished. Looking bright
Like the sun with all its colours and as hot as
The kiln to heat the potter's pots, its destiny is to
Kill, kill, kill!
She is gentle and is your inside heater that
Warms your heart. It lights up your life.
You can put your finger through it quickly and you
Won't feel a thing. It heats your food, smelling
Warm, hot and of the sweet food it is cooking.
You strike a match from the matchbox and
Watch it burn as the candle is lit from its source.
Hours later though, the bright, colourful flame
Has gone, died, and will never be seen again
Until another day when a new wick is once again lit.
Watch it as it shines. How can it live two lives?

Natalie Cooper (12)
Lutterworth High School

Fire

Brings comfort or catastrophe,
Crackles in the pits of Hell,
It can warm even the coldest of hearts,
Can burn in someone's heart as well,
Earth withers under its wrath,
The great Salamander in this is its home,
Forests, woods and trees fear its name,
Only one element it fears,
Crackling, spitting like a cobra,
All hypnotising colours red, orange, yellow
Cleverly hid the menace within,
Food bakes, fries and grills in it,
Bought life, brings life, takes life,
The smell or stench of smoke causes
The sirens of the world to scream,
All the members of the ember join as one,
The fire has now begun.

Elliot Hollingsworth (13)
Lutterworth High School

Fire Poem

It can roar but never speaks,
Its warmth is enjoyment,
Touch it and it leaves a mark,
Hot ashes from its trail,
The colours represent its personality,
Red represents its danger,
And yellow for its brightness it brings,
Its odour stays on your clothes and skin,
Until it's washed clean,
It brings life and also destroys,
A hate of many people,
An asset to others,
It can be put out by water,
Which calms and cools it,
It can be helping and fun,
It can be destroying and hurtful,
It can be hated and loved,
Some can be mesmerised by its flames,
The way it travels up and never goes down,
How it graduates and gets stronger,
And moves slowly but violently,
The sound it makes when it moves,
It cracks and collides with the wind,
And disintegrates leaves like small bugs,
So all that is left of it is the spine of the prey,
How it moves elegantly but fiercely,
And it destroys forests and wildlife,
When the fire strikes again.

Karla Bray (12)
Lutterworth High School

Fire

Reveals all within the darkness,
A wild flame completely uncontrolled
A roaring dragon hunting for food
Giving fear to all that gets in its way
Takes life or gives life to whom it chooses
A lonely soul waiting to strike

It flickers and spits
It changes its colour depending on its mood
Death or life it will choose
It will give light and guide you
It can be wild but it can be tamed

It roams and leaves a path of destruction
But could choose to stop at any time
A raging riot uncontrollable
Never to be stopped
Or a defenceless child only a month old
But in time it will grow

It will become strong again
And live up to its name
Unless it is put out.

Tom Taylor (13)
Lutterworth High School

Fire

It starts as a spark,
Then a huge shape,
Tinged with red,
Turning orange like the sun on a hot summer's day.
Pine needles crackling with laughter,
It spits with joy.
The flames roar and dance in the moonlight,
Reds, oranges, ambers flicker.
The sap hisses in the wood as the heat intensifies,
Sparks explode like fireworks in the sky.
The colours evolve into shades of blue,
As it starts to die down,
The fun runs away,
The dancing stands still,
The crackles and roars get quieter and quieter,
Until there's nothing left but the ashes,
Black dust surrounds you,
Everything's still,
It's totally silent.

Sarah Edgington (12)
Lutterworth High School

A Poem About Fire

The sun blazing on a warm summer's day.
The crackling noises it makes as it roars,
Spitting like an angry llama,
Killing people as it goes.
Billowing smoke as it rises,
Ever rising.
Strikes terror in people's hearts as it grows ever closer,
Smoke chokes as you inhale.
A real killer.
Fireworks exploding, leaving an array of sparks,
One big enemy.
Water douses as it is there, left to smoulder.
The day after all you see is the ash where the fire once lay,
Then it all blows away in a gust of wind.
The remains . . .
A large black patch,
As black as the night.
You sit there watching as it burns silently in the night sky,
As you sit in your sleeping bag eating marshmallows.

David Monk (13)
Lutterworth High School

Fire

Has no feelings, its heart is cold,
Spits like an angry cat,
Cackles with laughter.

Wood is its lifeline, its food,
When it is hungry it licks at its prey,
Trying to tempt it to join in its ways.

Great trees wither at the mere sight,
Getting engulfed in its treacherous arms,
Nowhere to hide.

Brave people bow before it,
Begging for pardon at its feet,
This powerful leader has no mercy.

It can also be a furnace, an oven or a kiln,
To give warmth, light or just company,
Its body becomes dazzling when the sun goes down.

This exceptional tool,
Is one that we must honour and respect,
If you don't, you are a fool.

Laura Heath (12)
Lutterworth High School

The World

Feel the world beneath your fingers and see,
See the sorrow, taste the faith,
Watch the hope and hear the pain,
Smell the willing, feel the trust,
Imagine dreams and taste the lust,
Feel the friendship and hear the hate,
Always be different, live to create.
Watch the leadership, feel the good,
Hear the hurt and smell the love.
Taste the suffering, feel the awareness,
Smell the power, live with fairness.
Taste the liberty, smell belief,
Hear support and sense the grief.
See equality, taste real life.
Smell the taking and hear the rights,
Taste the evilness, live to be free,
Smell the peace, hear humanity.
Sense the hunger, see the giving,
Remember the world in which we're living.

Jade Elliott (12)
Lutterworth High School

Wood

It can be sat on in many forms
Lovers kissing on a bench
Children working silently scribbling

It can be rings
Wedding, sapphire
Friendship, ruby

It can be climbed
Inch by steady inch
Step by steady step
Heave by steady heave

It can be used for poets, authors and scribes to write on
It can be used for poets, authors and scribes to write with

A useful resource used everywhere
Cargo
Lumbering
Cargo

It has friends and enemies
Yet it is not alive - it breathes
A life source

It can guard and be guarded

It stands
Fat and thin
Tall and small
Its hands waving in the breeze

Shelter yet death trap at a spark of a blade of light
It can die but when it does . . .
It screams . . .
Then falls
Dead as stone
Murdered by greed.

Emma Weston (12)
Lutterworth High School

The Ghost

One night I woke up with a start
After hearing a loud smash
I ran down the stairs
And saw a loud flash.

I saw a woman emerge
As the flash died down
I discovered she was a ghost
Wearing a long nightgown.

She was beautiful
Her lips were the colour of blood
Her neck was long and veined
And her hair was the colour of mud.

One night she dragged me out the door
To a faraway place
She pushed me roughly onto the floor
And violently hit me in my face.

I started to whimper
I started to cry
She pulled me out the window
And then she began to fly.

We flew into the dark
And flew around the stars
We sailed up the Milky Way
And circled around Mars.

We finally landed at my house
She tucked me into bed
And then apologised
For all the things she'd done and said.

Jemma Thomas (12)
Lutterworth High School

Water Poem

Flows down pipes,
Drops down drains,
Gushes down gutters,
Washes down windows,
Runs down rivers,
Trickles down streams,
Frosts, freezes and floods.
Clear as a crystal,
It reflects like a mirror,
Cold as ice,
Or as hot as fire.
Splash about in it,
Sink in it,
Swim in it,
And float in it,
Or even die in it!

Gemma Watson (12)
Lutterworth High School

Metal

He is shiny like a diamond,
He is cold like an ice cube and as smooth as glass,
He hides valuable possessions,
And bars away who know no good.
He transports people to faraway places,
And he probably is the most precious thing to man.

Without him our lives would be in despair,
His amazing strength knows no bounds,
The landscape towers above the ground,
Cold, dark, eerie, mysterious,
Feeds the wheels of industry,
Driving, grinding, churning,
Power in all its glory,
Strength beyond measure,
He is strong, solid and heavy.

Daniel Smalley (12)
Lutterworth High School

Fire

Red as congealed blood,
the colour of the death it brings.
Its breath is a flowing veil of darkness,
all life it consumes in its path.
Yet it is man's comrade,
an angel in the darkness.
In league with timber it stirs the blood,
devouring the cold with glee.
It's a towering beacon that leads the way
like a shooting star it parts the darkness.
It heats the body and warms the spirit,
when touched it leaves its brand.
The bane of wood and metal,
oxygen is its mate and water its foe.
It crackles like foil,
smells of ash,
and leaves a nauseating taste upon the tongue.

Harry Targett (12)
Lutterworth High School

Fire

It will scar for life
as bright as the sun
but the blueness is blinding
orange burning as red as a rose
turns frost into water
hot as an iron
it bends metal like rubber
smokes like a train
it's as warm as you want
it's fun but harmful
it will die out in time and it can be
calmed down with man's help.

Callum Hall (12)
Lutterworth High School

Fire

The silent killer gives no warning.
As it kills it brings life.
Powerful yet weak.
Water is its weakness.
But sometimes ignites.
Comes in many sizes and colours,
Burning blue,
Roasting red.
We love it when it is controlled,
But despise it when not.
Gives off a grey mist to make you choke.
A trail of destruction in its ashes.
In the cool it brings us warmth.
Guides us through the darkness.
Needs many things to light,
But easily done.
From a tiny glow to a bright light,
Its powerful energy fuels the world.

Matt Creasey (12)
Lutterworth High School

The Motorbikes
(Dedicated to Michael Blaney)

Like an Alpha wolf after a successful hunt
the bikes stand proud.
Their colours glistening in the sun
making white stripes of sunlight on the floor,
the engines are purring like a newborn kitten.
The bikes zoom down the road
like multicoloured lightning
and like fading black shapes
the bikes ride into the sunset.

Dan Liscombe (12)
Lutterworth High School

Concrete Jungle

Maze of asphalt and brick
Chimneys throw out pollution, blackening the sky
Buildings rise far above the streets, casting shadows
Drug-fuelled citizens speed past in metal machines of death
Chased by those that try to uphold the law, though they buckle
                                                    under the strain
Children cough poison fumes from their lungs, and walk
                              unguided through the bustling streets
There is a boss in the city, he sits behind a door marked 10
                              and distances himself from the outside world
To pass the time, he fabricates scandals and stories, so consuming
                                    they begin to seem real to him
War is waged on the streets, a car speeds past, a burst of gunfire
A man lies dying on the street, his blood forming a pool
Nobody stops to help
They bustle past and do not look down

A ring of lava surrounds the city.
Some know it as acheron - most refer to it as the M25.

David Mitchinson (13)
Lutterworth High School

The Sea

The sea is as blue as a clear sky on a summer's day.
It is as wild as a hungry dog.
It's so rough but so smooth.
It can take life but it can also give life.
You can travel on it.
It holds many mysteries.
It changes colour.
You can have fun with it.
It is a great resource.
It produces food.

Ian Dowler (12)
Lutterworth High School

Water

It flows down the river,
As calm as the sea,
It appears at the ocean,
Oh what could it be?

Liners, ferries, trawlers and yachts,
Sail on it day or night,
All sorts of fish live in it,
Whilst the moon reflects on it so bright.

It reaches to the Arctic,
And turns to ice,
Eskimos chop it up for their homes,
Slice by slice.

It falls from the heavens,
From right up high,
If you mix it with the sun,
Rainbows appear across the sky.

It flows out of the taps,
And into the sink,
Reach up to the cupboard and
Fill your glass with a healthy drink.

James Hughes (12)
Lutterworth High School

Fire

It does not feel pain,
But gives pain at your touch.
Orange swirls, red dances, yellow spits
And blue blinds.
Flickers in the moonlight,
Crackles in the mist,
Twists and turns in shadows,
Weaving in and out.
Keeps us warm at night through
Blizzards, storms, sleet or snow,
Or bitter cold chill winds that seem to
Blow and blow.
Glows in the morning, a pleasant,
Radiant shine,
Capturing the essence of the early sunrise.
A blazing kiln,
Of depths unknown,
Licking up the coal,
In a sea of deadly embers.
At the core of the Earth it rages with all its might,
Never resting because it helps keep the world alive.

Natasha Buck (12)
Lutterworth High School

The Lady Of The Air

The lady of the air,
That watches over me when I sleep,
Reads the thoughts around me,
No secrets I can keep.

She dives into my mind,
Leaving a misty, clotted state,
The silence lives no more,
Her arrogance I hate.

As quiet as the night,
As sly as a fox in day,
She hisses and swishes about my mind,
As in my bed I lay.

As the sun begins to rise,
My body begins to stir,
My eyes spring open as quick as a flash,
As all I can think of is her.

My eyes are squinted, my vision blurred,
As I wake again to life,
The atmosphere was so very tense,
You could slit it with a knife.

As I peer around my bedroom clutter,
All things are what they seem,
And then finally I realise
That she is only just my dream.

Emma Cluley (12)
Lutterworth High School

Rain

In the garden,
Enjoying the warm, bright sun,
Lying, lazing, lounging,
Soon the clouds cloak the sun,
Darkening the sky,
Dull, dead, dismal,
Then with one great gush,
It came pouring down,
Showering, soaking, splashing,
Making puddles on the pavement,
Growing slowly in time,
Rippling, running, rushing,
Flooding every empty gutter,
Trickling down every drain,
Flowing, falling, filling,
A cloud drifts,
Revealing a ray of sunlight,
Bright, blinding, beaming,
A sheet of blue hangs over me,
An arch of colour stands before,
Pink, purple, peach,
With a pot of gold,
Impossible to reach.

Natalie Roe (12)
Lutterworth High School

The Last Day

Death will creep into this world
People will die all shrivelled and curled
The light will turn to dark
And all the world will part

It will be the end
Everyone hopes it's pretend
It will be a nightmare
The devil will come out of its lair

War will begin
It will be a sin
We will die in pain
Everyone trying to be sane

As the sun goes down
People hear a screaming sound
The end of the world will be
In the year two thousand and sixty-three.

Toni Wright (13)
Lutterworth High School

Life

Life is a hall of mirrors
Or a Shakespeare play.
It is a puzzle
We face every day.
Full of challenges and regret.
A puzzle
That destiny has set.
Life is a curse to some,
Yet the end is feared by others.
Look and you'll see
A big difference between you and me.
I love my life no matter what goes wrong,
Because of my family.

Allen Carvin (12)
Lutterworth High School

Horse Show

Plaiting up with fumbling fingers,
Grooming up a polished shine,
Loading the lorry,
Driving by a quarry,
We draw near,
The excitement turning to fear,
As we look at the towering mountains faced in front,
The ones we were expected to jump.
In the warm-up ring I see faces like mine,
Anxious and pale like a wash of milk had come across our faces,
My turn in the ring,
Sit down to the beat of the canter,
Over the first, the second, we're clear!
The jumps now look tiny, as though they had been a tiger
                                                      reduced to a cub.
I entered the ring again to receive my fluttering first rosette.
I went to the lorry in a daze whilst people around me offered praise.
But I carried on to thank the one who did it all,
My horse.

Anna Greiff (12)
Lutterworth High School

My Bike

I went on my bike
To ride all day is what I like.

I like riding my bike
Because it's fun.

It's really nice when
I'm out in the sun.

Ricky Fryers (15)
Maplewell Hall Special School

The Chicken

The chicken is flickin' his feathers,
In all kinds of weathers.
He likes running around
Pecking and making sound.

He lives in a hen hut with others;
Where they can all be mothers.

They lay their eggs,
And kick their legs.

Running away they might try
If they can't they might fly.

Christopher Smith (15)
Maplewell Hall Special School

Science

Science is really good
Science is my best bud
Science should be really fun
I like it an absolute ton
Science is good and that is where I fit.

Eluned Bicknell (15)
Maplewell Hall Special School

Cats And Dogs

The cat tried to get fat,
the dog came to see the cat,
the cat tried to eat the dog,
and the dog sat on the mat,
so the cat jumped on the dog's hat.

Mindy Rakhra (15)
Maplewell Hall Special School

Is He Friend?

Is he friend
or is he foe?
He stood on my toe
because I went slow.
I get bubbles and I blow,
cos he likes to chase them so.
Yes he is my friend
although he drives me round the bend!

Louise Parker (15)
Maplewell Hall Special School

Untitled

I had a car, it didn't go far.
When I put my foot down,
It went like a clown.
My car looked like a sack of spuds.
It was covered in soap suds.
When my car broke down,
I looked like a clown.

Paul Mattox (15)
Maplewell Hall Special School

Things I Like

I like to go to school,
If I'm good I get to play pool.

I like to go to the youth club,
And sometimes I like to go to the pub.

I like to eat chips down the chip shop,
That is where I would like to stop.

Anne Marie Burrows (15)
Maplewell Hall Special School

Autumn

The wind blows the autumn leaves to the ground
They end up in a pile that looks like a mound.
The autumn leaves turn from green to brown.
That is when they fall down.

Daniel Murrell (16)
Maplewell Hall Special School

Karate Kid

Daniel does high kicks in karate,
This must make him a bit of a smartie.

He is called the Karate Kid,
Winning medals is what he did.

Daniel Hewitt (15)
Maplewell Hall Special School

The Greatest Man

Van Nistelrooy is a real top man
And I am his biggest fan.
They are a top club
And have some great subs.

Robbie Jamieson (15)
Maplewell Hall Special School

Untitled

I went to play football
On the astroturf
It is better in the hall
Football is great fun
When you're playing in the sun.

Tom Styles (16)
Maplewell Hall Special School

My Poem

The holocaust was a sad event,
Hitler's the one I do resent,
The Jews had done nothing wrong,
As this was where they did belong.

No freedom for the victims there,
They stood around totally bare,
Everyone with a glaring stare,
And the Nazis didn't even care.

I do forgive the Germans despite,
They killed the Jews with all their might,
I forgive but in my head,
I think of those that are now dead.

My feelings for the Jews remain the same,
I can feel their sorrow and their pain,
They suffered because of Hitler's views,
When it all ended, it was good news.

Carina Knox (13)
Mount Grace High School

Thoughts

I think about peaches
I think about cream
I think in class
People call it a daydream.

I think about ice
I think about mice
Some people think
That thinking is quite nice.

I think about nooks
I think about brooks
I think above rivers
And quivers and shivers.

Anna Robinson (12)
Mount Grace High School

Hitler And The Jews

He called his book 'My Struggle', but he never actually knew,
What it was like to be hated for something part of you.
It may have happened long ago, but the pain's still raw and red,
For if it wasn't for this man, 6 million people would not be dead.

You can't say it never happened, these people didn't just disappear,
It would be ignorant to forget, these people lived in fear,
They were pieces on his chessboard, there for just his needs,
But when it came to the killing, other people did his deeds.

It will never go away, always playing a part in my mind,
The horror that has happened cannot be left behind.

I feel a sense of sorrow now, but this is what I know,
It would be different if it were my family, no forgiveness I could show.
But they're all together now, no more suffering, no more pain,
The world has stood up and said the Jews were not to blame.

I can't imagine what it felt like to be marched towards your death,
Knowing that you were going to die,
And that running would be useless.
I think Anne Frank summed it up when I her diary she wrote,
'And all because they're Jews'.

So please, *everyone*, take note.

Holly Kemp (13)
Mount Grace High School

A Poem About Life

L iving in this world with others around you,
   Liking your friends and hating your foes.
I f you didn't have a life you wouldn't be here,
   If you didn't have others you would be alone.
F eelings and thoughts make your life interesting,
   For if you had no thoughts and feelings your life would be empty.
E verything on this planet, in this world,
   Everything in this universe has got a life of its own.

Sarah Shreeve (12)
Mount Grace High School

Have You Ever Looked Into The Sky?

Have you ever looked up into the sky
To see acres of fluffy white clouds floating by?
Soar up in an aeroplane just like a gull
Viewed from above they could be cotton wool
A puppy, an elephant, what can you see?
The clouds make the shapes you want them to be.

When I look up in the sky
I see clouds floating by
I dream of mermaids swimming under the sea
Twisting and turning gracefully
Sheep, cows and horses graze on a farm
A beautiful puppy jumps into my arms
A forest, a mountain, a beautiful house
An enormous giant, a minuscule mouse
Have you ever looked up into the sky
And dreamed a dream as the world floated by?

Hannah Godrich (12)
Mount Grace High School

Sunset

Sunset is a mix of colours
which dips into a blanket of blue ribbon
as the sun sinks lower and lower
the sky turns an angry red
like blood spilt from God in the sky

Sunset is dull but amazing
the lights and colours light up
the sky one last time, then
all goes dark and shiny
as the stars light up the night sky.

Amy Tyrrell (11)
Mount Grace High School

Easter Island Poem

E aster Islanders were so asinine,
A s they killed their population one by one. They
S tructured statues made of stone which stood
T owering over them, representing their ancestors.
E aster Islanders worshipped them as their god. Easter Island was a
R egal place with food everywhere,

I ncluding fish from the sea,
S o it seemed like paradise, but
aL as, all the food went
A nd because they were so obsessed with building statues,
N ever would they survive.
D own went the trees, one after

A nother. They couldn't build canoes to escape because of
                                        their foolishness.
L eft on Easter Island, stranded!
L onging to get out,

G oing nowhere, but wars were breaking
O ut. These Polynesian people were coming to an end!
N ever thought about anything else, that's why their civilisation
                                        came to an

E nd!

Condemn the statues!

Nicola Roper (13)
Mount Grace High School

Return To The Camp

How did it happen that I survived
And yet so many others died?
Sometimes we hoped, sometimes we tried,
Sometimes we broke down and we cried.
We lost our dignity and sold our souls,
We buried our people in deep dark holes.
We burned their bodies late at night,
It truly was a terrible sight.
The smell of death was in the air,
They took our clothes and cut our hair.
Each day was lived in fear and dread,
They gave us water and stale bread.
Our lives were just a living hell,
The rest I just can't bear to tell.

And now I have come back again,
To see if I can ease the pain.
I wonder just what was his game,
And what did Hitler think he'd gain?
And as I stand here at the gate,
I never understood my fate.
At last I weep, at last I cry,
But I'll never ever understand *why*.

Keira Miller (13)
Mount Grace High School

Am I The One?

Am I the one who doesn't eat?
Am I the one who doesn't like meat?
Am I the one who kills a dove?
Am I the one who doesn't believe there's one above?
Am I the one who doesn't take part?
Am I the one who has the weak heart?
Am I the one who cannot spell?
Am I the one who will go to Hell?
Am I the one who won't be rich?
Am I the one not on the football pitch?
Am I the one who's from another land?
Am I the one who doesn't give a helping hand?
Am I the one who always kills?
Am I the one who steals from the tills?
Am I the one who will never die?
Am I the one who will always lie?
Am I the one with the nice car?
Am I the one who won't go very far?

. . . Am I the one who won't eat ham?
Or am I just the one I am?

Nisur Nadar (13)
Redmoor High School

The Sunflower

I grew a giant sunflower
That started from a tiny seed
It grew and grew and grew
Next to a lot of weeds
Out of the top
There came a pop
As a flower waved in the breeze.

Kerry Exon (11)
Shepshed High School

Autumn

The leaves crunch like crusty bread
Covered in golden syrup
Squirrels squabble around the cold, bare trees
Hedgehogs hibernate in their nests

The wind whistles, whirling wildly
Emerald-coloured holly bushes with glistening red rubies
Swaying in the cold autumn wind
Beautiful, bold blackberries bursting with purple juice

Pumpkins prowl like the pretty Pink Panther
Wasps sleepwalk, crashing into brick-hard houses
Harvest festivals are everywhere you look
Though the only colours you can see are ruby, amber,
                                     bloodstone and garnet

Conkers lying on the ground like pebbles on a beach
Children shouting, screaming and chasing the golden, crunchy leaves
Butterflies spread their wings like wild fairies.

Astin Storer (11)
Shepshed High School

Life

What is life, work or play?
How long will we be here? It could be years or a day.
Do we all find love or is it just for some?
People always say your time will come.
Will I have a good job and a close friend?
Will I have money and love or will my dreams come to an end?
I can't predict the future, my dreams I have many,
Which one will come true? It could be one of any.

Cassie Soars (12)
Shepshed High School

The Egg That Caused Mayhem

It was a sunny day in Billagong when the postman came to call,
He rattled on the letterbox like a stampede going by.
He left a tiny cardboard box which said *Fragile* on the top,
And when I opened it a little egg I'd got.

It sizzled and it shook and made the most awful noises,
And then the egg began to break,
Crack, crinkle, crunch,
And then it hatched.

It was an ugly kind of creature,
With black spots on its back.
It was as green as a frog,
And had fangs like Dracula.

We fed it every day as it ate a lot,
On leaves and lettuce and lamb.
It got bigger and bigger as it ate so much,
And at last he ran and ran and he was gone.

He ripped up trees like a stick in the ground,
And started hundreds of fires.
He was as strong as five elephants put together,
And he roared and he rumbled as he rampaged through the town.

Parliament heard and sent out the army,
To catch this wild beast.
With nets and nails and Nutella to tempt the creature away,
He now lives in Billagong Zoo, as happy as a dragon can be.

Chloe Jones (11)
Shepshed High School

Autumn

When the autumn comes, the leaves turn bronze, golden and amber,
In the woods the holly berries are big, red, ripe rubies,
In the park there are golden conkers with spiky, sharp shells,
In the autumn the leaves crunch like the pebbles on a beach,
In the woods the wind is howling like a big, hungry wolf.

Ryan Locke (11)
Shepshed High School

There's A Dragon Outside This House

Last night I looked out of my window
And staring back at me was a dragon
Its hair was a row of jagged, fiery mountains
Pointing to the sky
On top of its head sat a horn
It was smooth, sharp, shiny and scary-looking
Its ears were like a paper doily folded in half
It had great big eyes like mouldy eggs with green yolk
Its nostrils were like two silver rings
Sitting on the end of its nose

Its long, lean, lanky neck was like a giraffe's
Its neck led to two short, stumpy and stubby arms
Its belly was round and yellow like a sun on its blue body
Its legs were like brackets with feet
Its tail was a slithery, scaly snake, swishing
And best of all it was smiling and waving at me!

Rachael Burton (10)
Shepshed High School

Dragon Poem

A scaly, dark red dragon,
Sat gleaming in the sun.
His long spiky golden tail curled round
On the dusty ground.

His eyes were as dark as coal,
And he had wings and
Shocking great white fangs.
He had a fearsome fiery flame
Which came out his gruesome nose.

He looked really big and scary,
But deep inside he's just
A harmless, old red dragon,
Who's scared of a tiny mouse?

Chelsea Davies (11)
Shepshed High School

Autumn

The wind is like a howling wolf
At midnight, as if in pain,
The children playing in the leaves,
Jumping round all excited.

Bonfire Night has come quickly,
Everyone has got their guy ready,
The fire is as bright as the burning sun,
It's as hot as an erupting volcano.

The hedgehog is getting ready to hibernate,
Collecting food for his very long sleep.
The birds are starting to fly off,
Flying to a hotter country.

Purply-pink precious berries
Have come out into the cold autumn air,
Squirrels collecting nuts and berries,
As the whole of nature prepares to sleep.

Luke Eggleston (11)
Shepshed High School

Autumn

In the autumn the leaves crunch like crusty bread,
The wind whistles, whirling,
Emerald-coloured holly bushes glittering with red rubies,
Sway in the cold autumn air.
Squirrels scurry slowly round the bare trees,
Beautiful bold blackberries burst with juice,
Pumpkins prowl like the Pink Panther along the street.
Wasps sleepwalk and crash into brick-hard houses,
Harvest festivals are everywhere you look,
Though the only colours you can see are ruby, amber,
                                    bloodstone and garnet.

Georgia Bennett (10)
Shepshed High School

Autumn

In autumn the leaves are
like different coloured jewels
falling from the sky.

The wasps are like dizzy
drivers, crashing into
flower pots and walls.

The squirrels run past
as they collect their nuts
for the winter stock.

As you walk down the street
you see pumpkins pulling
funny faces through the window.

The wind howls like a screaming tornado
you come home from school and it is getting dark already
as the night comes earlier in autumn.

Katie Hutchinson (11)
Shepshed High School

Stars

(Dedicated to Great Uncle Ivor)

The stars above are sparkling lights in the night sky
Big in size, small in sight, dancing and twinkling forever bright
Reach out and catch a falling star
For in each is love
The most powerful magic
Look outside, up above
There are stars outside, each with love.

Bethan Johnson (11)
Shepshed High School

Passing Time

The skies are blue
The Earth is round
It is like a ball that
Goes around and around.

It passes the sun
To make it light
As time goes by
It passes the moon
To make it dark.

The dull red shine of Mars
Shines close to the
Bright light of the stars.

The sparkly shine of the stars
Reflects on the green and blue ball
It glows brightly
In the moonlight.

Christopher Davis (12)
Shepshed High School

The Dragon

The dragon had spiky, scaly spikes on his skin.
They were as sharp as a shark's tooth.
Out of his nostrils came flashing, fiery flames,
Falling as fast as the fastest rocket.
His teeth are tremendous and terribly twisted.

The dragon breathes out blistering, burning flames.
He bellows out flames as high as any volcano.
His eager, evil eyes staring at his dinner.
He strides huge steps towards his prey
Who is crouching like a frightened animal
Behind a rock because that prey is me.

Georgina Wilson (11)
Shepshed High School

Autumn

As autumn comes, the colours break through.
Leaves fall down like bombs in slow motion,
Red, yellow, brown and orange too,
Together a fountain of colour.

Conkers, all spiky, fall from their perch.
They are prisoners, trapped in confinement,
Until a child lets them free,
And their shiny, silky skin is revealed.

A wasp hovers, half asleep, nibbling
On the insides of a juicy apple,
And blackberries are picked one by one,
Each is an exploding landmine of juice.

The branches wave to one another.
The wind is their only energy.
Then, as the wind slowly dies down,
They stand peacefully in light stillness.

Finally, as the wind starts to howl
Hungrily, like a small, helpless wolf,
It makes small whirlwinds with the leaves,
As only the wind is awake.

Hayley Mabe (11)
Shepshed High School

My Dragon

My dragon is a ferocious, feisty fighter
Who gnaws and gnashes on gullible knights like a gruesome beast!
He's an enormous snake with arms and legs
Who's slimy, slippery, spiky and spotty!
He roars, rumbles and rants like a gigantic bear.
His cave smells of burnt black buttered toast!
My red-eyed, green-scaled, fire-breathing dragon!

Neha Puntambekar (11)
Shepshed High School

Smile

Smiling is infectious, you catch it like the flu,
When someone smiled at me today,
I started smiling too.

I passed around the corner,
And someone saw my grin.
When he smiled I realised,
I'd passed it onto him.

I thought about that smile,
Then I realised what it's worth.
A single smile just like mine,
Could travel round the Earth.

So if you feel a smile begin,
Don't leave it undetected.
Let's start an epidemic quick,
And get the world infected!

Sean Pell (11)
Shepshed High School

A Fire Breather

This dragon's stare can knock you out.
This dragon's eyes are like nothing you've seen.
This dragon's scales are as rough as sandpaper.
When you stare at him you feel as if your life has flashed before you.
His fire is as hot as the sun.

Be careful of his long snake-like tail that can snap you like a whip.
Watch out for his glistening eyes like the moon.
Tiptoe past him with his lion-like roar.
His whole body towers above you and you feel like a shrivelled mouse.
You try to run away but it's too late, his jaws snap shut.

Laura Francis (11)
Shepshed High School

My Dragon

My dragon is gruesomely greasy, gross and giant
Like a smelly, slimy, scaly, soggy reptile
It has big teeth, as big as frost falling off a cliff
My dragon crackles as he walks, cracking his bones
And crunching little mice with his fangs
He smells like black, burnt, buttered toast
As he strolls by you
For his lunch he tears trembling pteranadon triplets
For his tea.

Siân Plummer (11)
Shepshed High School

My Dragon

My dragon breathes ferocious, fiery
flames that corrupt souls of his victims.
He has a tremendous, terrorising tail to
trash all beings that face him in battle.
His crunching claws can crush castles.
The scales on my dragon are like iron.

Lewis Brown (11)
Shepshed High School

Seetal

Seetal is sweet as sugar,
Ripe and bubbly,
A league of her own,
Seetal is extravagant,
She is the best from the rest.

Seetal Patel (11)
The Garendon High School

The Sea

Seagulls soar overhead,
People play in the sand on the shore,
Running in and out, splashing, jumping, laughing,
Slippery seaweed underfoot.
Sun, high in the light blue sky makes the sea shimmer
Like a thousand diamonds.
Boats bouncing and bopping against the waves,
Playful or is it menacing?
The water pounds like a lion onto the shore.

Beneath the waves a new world awaits,
Corals, city to many creatures of the deep.
Colourful fish dart to and fro, minding their own business,
As above the day goes by.

At night the people may go and the darkness comes,
But the sea never rests, its energy is constant and it's never alone.
Look carefully and you may see the images of ghostly ships
Claimed by moody waters.

Charlie Craggs (11)
The Garendon High School

The Sea!

The sea! The sea! The open sea,
the blue, the fresh, the ever free,
it is where it will always be,
with the blue above and the blue, below.

Lots of seaweed can be seen
floating on top
and big waves roll all day long
and splash against the rocks.

Megan Spencer aka Kirk (11)
The Garendon High School

The Vampire

Running through the forest,
Dodging round the trees,
Harry was trembling,
Shaking at his knees.

The vampire was closing,
Nearer and nearer he came,
His fangs dripping with blood,
His eyes all aflame.

Harry saw a cottage ahead,
And ran as fast as he could,
With the vampire close behind him,
Racing through the wood.

He was caught inside the kitchen,
And thrown into the pot,
The vampire chopped up the veg,
Things were getting hot.

That was the end of poor Harry,
Casseroled in the pot,
A tasty meal for a vampire,
Whether he liked it or not.

Daniel Hurrell (13)
The Garendon High School

The Sea

The sea is as rough as a hurricane,
With a horrible, salty, gritty taste,
But nevertheless refreshing,
The sea is like a giant Hoover,
Eating up everything in its path,
The sea is always wishing to play . . .

David Mortimer (12)
The Garendon High School

The Sea!

The sea is sometimes like a hungry lion,
Waiting for its dinner.
It crashes and splashes and roars and moans,
But it just seems to get thinner and thinner.

'Til one morning in April or May,
It would be so calm.
You'd just wanna pick it up,
And it would just sit there in your palm.

The sea is like a vicious bear,
Waiting for the kill.
It would knock down a ship,
Guilty, it would lie there very, very still.

But on an icy winter's night,
It would glisten in the frosty moon.
Along would come an evil cloud,
And the sea would crash and splash and roar and moan,
All the way till noon!

But the sea is like a friend to me,
A buddy it will always be,
It might crash and splash and roar and kill,
But the sea will always be a great friend to me!

Daryl-Hannah Webster (11)
The Garendon High School

The Sea

When the stormy rain comes at night
The sea, outraged, begins to fight
Without a care it *crashes* and *bangs*
Like vampires it has sharp, jagged fangs.

But when the sun starts to rise
The sea calms down, it almost dies.

Yasmin Mahboubi (11)
The Garendon High School

The Earth

The Earth is big, round and great,
on this Earth it's just me and my mate,
we go to the shops,
and buy lollipops,
on this Earth that's big, round and great.

The Earth has many a thing,
but I ask, where are the kings?
There's only a queen,
well that's all I've seen,
on this Earth where there's many a-thing.

The Earth has many a season,
and for that there's many a reason,
there's summer, autumn, winter and spring,
there must be a reason, I know there's something,
on this Earth that has many a season.

The Earth is big, round and great.
Oh no . . . got to dash, I'm late!

Alana Spencer (11)
The Garendon High School

The Sea

The sea crashes over the pretty rock pools,
Giving the creatures a refreshing splash, nice and cool.

Sometimes it's quiet and sometimes it's loud,
But it must always make the sea creatures proud!

If you go right down to the sea's toes,
You will find fish like colourful rainbows.

But lurking in the slippery, slimy seaweed,
Is a ravenous shark ready to feed!

When the night is finally here,
The dolphins leap in the sea, crystal clear!

Helen Jasmin Orr (11)
The Garendon High School

Paradise Island

I'm on an island,
Far away,
Surrounded by water,
Surrounded.

I look up and see,
A blazing, bright sun,
A diamond reflection worth a thousand pounds,
The glistening, shimmering, sparkling ball of fire.

I see the sea,
A crystal reflection of me,
Shimmering, turquoise diamonds,
And a ripple, stir, flutter and flow.

I walk down the beach,
Shiny, sleek, silky sand,
Hear the gentle, tranquil sound,
As the water hits the shore,
The calm, peaceful, placid pacific.

As the sun goes down there's a gentle breeze,
Slow, calm and soothing,
Feel it brush your face and ruffle your hair,
Soothing, soothing, soothing.

I see the palm trees,
Let branches wave free,
Flutter, flap and sway,
Waving all troubles away.

I'm on paradise island,
Far away,
Crystal, turquoise water,
Bright, blazing sun,
Gentle, soothing breeze,
Soft, silky sand,
And tall palm trees,
Surrounded by pleasure,
Surrounded.

Andrea Cooper (11)
The Garendon High School

The Sea

The sea is like a rogue,
Foraging through the lands.
It sucks in what it can find,
And devours it in the dark, dingy depths.

The sea looks like a giant,
Big and tough,
Crashing and clashing,
Against the cliff all day.

The touch of the sea,
Is like a glass of water,
On a hot sunny day, cold and refreshing.
The touch of the sea,
Is lovely to me.

The sea is like a rogue,
Foraging through the land,
When he's found what he wants,
He rests on the sand.

Joshua Davis (11)
The Garendon High School

The Sea

The sea is like a magical pond
Never going away,
And when the children come to play
All the seagulls fly away.

The sea is splashing day and night
Giving children quite a fright,
Then, everyone goes to sleep
And all you can hear is the tiniest beep.

Oliver Turton (11)
The Garendon High School

A Torturer's Death

A sick woman lies in a prison bed,
A glass of cold water by her side.
Holding her rosary she sighed and said,
'I know how the children felt when they died.'

The blonde-haired woman had stood in the dock,
With her dark-haired partner by her side.
Tapes were played of tortures enacted -
She relived those moments with pride.

Now comes a dark man with a dog collar on,
The pale-faced woman coughs and is shriven.
He sits on her bed and reflects on her sin,
And absolution at last is given as last rites are given.

He listened to her as she said,
'I feel that I'm going to Heaven.'
Hours after that she was dead,
Her body is guarded; is her soul in Heaven?

Belinda Edney (14)
The Garendon High School

Poppy (Hamster)

I've got a cheeky hamster.
Her name is Pop or Poppy.
She's soft and fluffy and we cuddle her a lot.
She's white, brown and coffee.
When she eats
She has big, puffy cheeks.
She often gets away,
But she comes back another day.

Sean Erskine (12)
The Garendon High School

F1

All the colours of Formula One, like chocolates in a box
Lined up on the grid as smart as soldiers on parade.
To start the race the red lights beam.
Deafening as the pistons roar like thunder.

Ferrari as red as a scarlet rippling ribbon,
Braking into corners like a cheetah catching its prey.
Pit stop! Screeching brakes, mechanics swarm like ants.
Schumacher exits the pit lane like a bat out of Hell . . .

Viciously attacking the chicane like a rottweiler,
Impatiently overtaking the back markers.
The chequered flag's in sight,
Flies across the finish line like a greyhound.

Jack Price (12)
The Garendon High School

The Sea

The sea is like a sparkling chandelier,
Glistening in its open space,
Shining and lighting up the world
With its style and its grace.

The sea loves crashing against the rocks,
It doesn't care if it gets hurt badly,
It shines and glitters all day,
I look at it very sadly.

Now this is the end of my poem,
I hope you have enjoyed,
I liked writing it,
As much as I enjoyed.

Roshun Lakha (11)
The Garendon High School

Angels

The angels sing at Heaven's doors,
Our spirits live on forever.
Your heart rebounds inside my soul,
Our hearts are united together.

My head spins round in anger,
The frustration rips out my heart.
Not for us to be together,
But for us to be apart.

You'll be in my heart forever and on,
Your soul will be joined to mine.
My love and only you will see,
We will be united in time.

You are the angel wrapping me tight,
Keeping me warm night after night.
Looking over me day after day,
Sending my fears and troubles away.

Megan Griffiths (12)
The Garendon High School

Kirk Legs It

Space, the final front ear
Captain Kirk certainly nose
That if he goes too far
He might not get back ear .

But if he has the cheek
And doesn't come to 'arm
He might go for a day or two
Or he might just go for a week.

Andrew Danby Knight (11)
The Garendon High School

Minotaur

In the basement of the palace,
was a maze,
a dark maze,
a cold maze,
twisting, turning,
round and round,
walls covered in dust,
and cobwebs hanging off,
rolling bones leading to the Minotaur,
plod, roar
plod, roar
plod, roar,
the hairy, horny Minotaur,
clashing the rotting skeleton together,
boulders rolling down,
with blood dripping off,
the dark maze,
the cold maze,
twisting, turning, turning, turning,
never ending . . .

Emily Brailsford (11)
The Garendon High School

The Sea

T oday I'm going to watch the sea, just my friend and me.
H oping that there's lots of new,
E xciting things for us to do.

S am now knows how to swim.
E ven though it's time to go
A nd head for home.

Layton Weston (11)
The Garendon High School

The Sea

The sea is a wild pig,
Giant and rough,
Washing up and down on the
Trickly stones.

The sea is a big bully, big and hard,
Rushing on the seashore,
Giant and grey,
Rippling on the slippery sand.

The sea is a fun place,
Where people come and play,
The waves slapping
Up and down on their tanned legs.

Vishantji Odedra (11)
The Garendon High School

Tigger

All my cat does is sleep and eat -
but he's strong and brave - he's sniffed Mum's feet!

Because he's like a crocodile,
Tigger has the widest smile!

He eats his Whiskas, being quiet -
but he should be on a diet.

He may be very fat -
but Tigger is the best cat.

When it comes to cats - Tigger's the king,
cos he's the best at everything!

Mark Boyde-Shaw (11)
The Garendon High School

My Mate Jamie

I have a mate called Jamie,
His personality's flamy,
He's absolutely great,
Cos he's my mate.

Jamie's mates with me you see,
He is really cool with me,
He's really slick,
And he is not thick.

I like his hat,
He likes my cat,
We hardly play out,
Cos he's never about.

Jamie's mates with me you see,
He is really cool with me,
He's really slick,
And he is not thick.

He burps loads,
He likes toads,
This mate of mine,
We'll be mates for all time.

Jamie's mates with me you see,
He is really cool with me,
He's really slick,
And he is not thick.

The way he laughs is like a sign,
To say that he's a mate of mine,
I really like Jamie, I really do, *ha!*
Don't make fun, *cos he'll get ya!*

Emma Peach (11)
The Garendon High School

The Sea

I was walking along the pier one day
When I noticed something not far away.
As I walked intrigued to where it lay,
I thought for a second I heard it say:

>   You cannot see
>   The whole of me,
>   For I am the shiny sea
>   Hear the children shout, 'Yipee!'

I saw dreamy dolphins diving in the deep, dark cover,
Acting as though the sea was their mother.
It's a shame they haven't got a brother,
But they will always have a dear, sweet lover.

Tickly, twirly tentacles of an octopus,
For octo-children there's always a fuss!
To get the children anywhere there's nothing to suss,
The eight pounding arms are like seats for a bus!

The thrashing sea was as cold as ice,
Rushing around like millions of dice!
To get completely soaked is my advice,
Cos on a hot summer's day the water feels so nice!

There were loads of different kinds of fish,
The tuna and salmon looked quite delish!
Those two are my favourite dish,
But there is one thing that I really wish.

I wish there was no litter,
Lying on the ground.
Then the brightly coloured sea,
Would he happy all year round!

So to everyone out there,
Stop throwing litter please!
If you want to know why,
Just do the same as me.

And look in the dark water
At all the dead fish floating around,
And make everyone around you happy,
As there's no litter to be found.

Jade Hassall (11)
The Garendon High School

A Christmas Tree

I really think it would be a boring life for a Christmas tree.
Standing there, waiting around,
Just for someone to chop you down.
To be tied up in a net,
Then stuck on a car is quite a fret.
Driven off to a new abode,
And planted in the living room, all alone.
Then the time comes to be dressed up,
Covered in shiny stuff.
Then after new year, you get chucked away,
To rot outside for the rest of your days.

Ben Wall (12)
The Garendon High School

Ladder

I climbed up the ladder,
right up to the top,
I stepped off the ladder,
and fell right through the clouds.

My head landed in a vice,
someone turned the handle,
and now my head is a rectangle,
and I've also got square eyes.

Antony Pyatt (11)
The Garendon High School

The Ghost Ship

One cold and blustery winter night,
I stand alone on an empty pier.
The lapping waves are soothing me,
They're washing away my fear.

The moon is gleaming like a silver ball,
Hung in the misty sky.
It's shimmering like the coiling sea,
Its beauty caught my eye.

As I listen to the beauteous sea,
I hear a muffled cackling.
To my left, sitting on a boat,
I see a sea merchant laughing.

'What's so funny?' I asked him now,
He looks up and catches my eye.
'Let me tell you a story of a ship,'
And he gives a muffled sigh.

'Legends say and legends tell,
Of a ghost ship named after Lydia Rose,
Who drifts upon these open shores,
Seeking the crew it used to know.

Seven hundred years ago,
It sunk because of a leak in the bow.
They tried mending the enormous hole,
Why it leaked, no one knows how.

The ship sank and now they're all lost,
Believed to be under the waves.
500 men together I think,
Nestled in their watery graves.'

As I listen to this chilling tale,
Flooding through my hazy head.
I turn sharply on my heel,
'I'm going home,' I say.

But as I look up to the stars above,
A dense, foggy mist is covering the sea.
It's forming the shape of a pirate ship,
I can't believe what I can see!

A cold and dark shiver runs up my spine,
Was this the ship I'd been told about?
Were the blood-curdling tales really true?
I guess I'm about to find out.

Written across the side of the boat,
Was the name, 'The Lydia Rose'.
Its flag flutters dauntlessly in the wind,
My mounting fears grow and grow.

It sails along the snappy sea,
Unflinching in its stride it goes.
I hear a shrill scream from the deck of the boat,
This is the way ghost stories go!

My heart's racing and my legs are stiff,
I have to get out of here.
I turn to the sea merchant for some help,
But find he has disappeared.

But as the clouds fade slowly away,
And the moon breaks through the desolate night,
The ghost ship slowly disappears,
It's certainly given me a fright.

As I stand on the edge of the pier,
I look out onto the dazzling sea.
I wonder if what just happened is true,
It surely has petrified me.

One cold and blustery winter night,
I stand alone on an empty pier.
The lapping waves are soothing me,
They're washing away my fear.

Hannah Bailey (12)
The Garendon High School

My Cat Joe

My cat's name is Joe,
He does not wear a bow,
He always wants a biscuit,
So he might explode, so please Joe don't risk it.

Joe is brown with a bit of ginger,
But he is not a very big whinger,
He is really fluffy,
He is sometimes very scruffy.

He sits under my bed,
He sometimes bumps his head,
He sits in the sink,
But he never has a drink.

Stacey Hodgett (11)
The Garendon High School

The Hurricane

The wind, like a lion roaring,
Its flaming energy, in its body storing!
The path it blows up,
Was like smashing a cup!
It feeds on power,
Stronger it becomes, shunting the flowers!
Its destructive personality,
Is a hazardous formality!
It throws itself carelessly,
The energy it had stored had blasted out ferociously!

Jordan Makwana (11)
The Garendon High School

The Fiery Pits Of Hell Rise Again!

Molten rock surrounding me,
Earth crumbling before me,
Exploding guisers of the world,
The screeching screams of the forbidden world,
The burning flesh of man,
The brimstone above me,
I feel the heat and death.

Malick Attenborough (11)
The Garendon High School

The Sea

Sand like a handful of gritty, crunchy, salty sugar,
It feels like a wet, warm, salty Slush Puppy.
The sea is like a witch's poison with beachy smells,
From far out in the salty, sickly, slimy seaweed sea,
You can see the crooked cliffs crashing and crumbling
To the depths of the ocean.

Daisy-Mae Willumsen (11)
The Garendon High School

The Dark Woods

The wood all creepy and dark,
Some glowing eyes staring at me.
An owl wooing in the dark,
The wind is whistling in my ears.
A faint smell of a cat or a dog,
A smell of burning bark and wood.
I feel strange and lonely here in the dark.

Elizabeth Green (11)
The Garendon High School

A Winter Evening

Two lovers together
Now they're apart
Since that stormy night.

As they stood,
Hand in hand,
Watching the white-globe moon.

A tiny creek,
A silent groan,
The young lovers are unaware.

Then the rotting timbers
Suddenly drop
Into the ice-cold waves below.

Their screams are not heard
Through the crashing, smashing breakers.
One boy, one girl, doomed.

And the freezing water
Closes over,
The wood sinks to the ocean floor.

As he plays
With the unlucky couple
Clawing and throwing them with his lethal paws

He is not hungry
Just in the mood
For washing the couple with his frosty showers.

Then as the lovers
Slowly lose their will
To go on in these helpless waters

The sea decides
He is too tired
To play with these people anymore

So he drops them
Down into the icy depths
Slowly, silently, still.

Rosamund Piper (11)
The Garendon High School

Being A Tree

What a boring life it would be,
to stand around like a tree.
For years and years they stand around,
waiting for a certain time to come,
when a man will come and hack them down.

The best you can hope for in the afterlife,
is to become a Christmas tree.
You stand around in a great big store,
until you're sold to a jolly fat man.

They dress you in fancy lights,
then on the day after Christmas,
Deathday as it's known to us trees.
They strip you of your flashy lights,
and kick you out to rot all night.
So if I was a tree, I wouldn't stick around,
I'd sprout some legs and run like mad.

Denis Njiru (11)
The Garendon High School

Monster!

It's hairy, it's scary
It thumps and it bumps
It smashes and it crashes
Quick, run away

It's freaky, it's shrieky
It's coming, it's running
It's roaring, it's snoring
Wherever should I hide?

It's creeping, but leaping
It's squelching but belching
It's growling but howling
Suddenly it ends . . .

Georgina Clayton (11)
The Garendon High School

City Vs United

The players come out onto the pitch,
The crowd scream, 'Come on United,'
The referee blows his whistle,
Off they go and the crowd get excited.

A tackle goes in,
The ref says, 'A foul.'
He shows him red,
And off he goes.

The free-kick is taken,
It curls around the wall,
The goalie dives and misses,
A *goal* for United.

The half-time whistle goes,
With the score 1-0 to United,
The crowd scream again,
Except for the City fans.

The second-half kicks off,
City straight on the attack,
A brilliant ball across the pitch,
A cracking shot was that.

City run into the box,
A sliding tackle takes them down,
The ref says, 'Penalty,'
And then sends the player off.

The ball is put on the spot,
The taker runs towards the ball,
He shoots and scores,
City now 2-1 up.

City running down the right wing,
United tackle them as City fans sing,
A tremendous cross into the box,
United are now level.

Going into the last seconds,
A free ball in the centre,
United get to the ball first and shoot,
A goal for United.

The final whistle blows,
A win for United,
Their fans scream and shout,
United 3, City 2 in the way the score goes.

Seven Bajot (11)
The Garendon High School

My Teacher's An Alien

My teacher's an alien
Yes, my teacher's an alien
You can tell by her eyes
Her eyes are so big and green
With gunge coming out when she cries.

Her head's the shape of an egg
Oh and have I told you she's got three heads?

She has green hair
Oh and she has antennas
Coming out the top of her head.

Her nose is long and pointy
And has bogies and snot
Coming out.

And that describes my alien teacher.

Danielle Mitchell (11)
The Garendon High School

My Little Fan

My little fan is a hurricane,
I put it on two and it blows me to Timbuktu,
So I told my friends
I could do good deals on holidays.
I've called myself, Fan Air,
And now I am a billionaire.

Stefan Scutt (11)
The Garendon High School

The Spook Of Hallowe'en

A daring little creepy spider
creeps among the cracks,
the creaks and cracks
and snaps and claps
echo round the room.
As you step outside you hear inside
the sound of the scrape of a paw,
the sound of distant footsteps
and the slam of a distant door.

Petra Baker (11)
The Garendon High School

The Sea

T he sea is wild like a lion,
H igh waves clash against the rocks,
E veryone is enjoying themselves.

S andcastles getting washed away,
E very child is getting upset,
A dults are trying to rebuild them as fast as they can.

Crash!

Richard Squires (12)
The Garendon High School

The Sea

T he sea is like a soft blue liquid.
H ave loads of fun so you play along.
E at ice cream beside the bench.

S ee the sparkled, shiny blue sea
E ndless sand is all you can see.
A te my ice cream, now it's time to have a swim.

Ajay Patel (11)
The Garendon High School

The Sea

The deep, dark sea
Is chilly and cold,
Freezing and bitter

Whoosh! Whoosh!

The wild, sinister sea
Always leaping and swaying,
Crashing and bashing

Whoosh! Whoosh!

The murky, mysterious sea
Continuous and thunderous,
Wailing and roaring

The boisterous, mysterious sea

Just like me!

Kane McCaughie (11)
The Garendon High School

The Sea

The sea is like a raging dog,
It's rough at times but is often calm.
The sand is like a blanket over
A dog sleeping when it's still.
Most of the time in the morning
The dog can't see from the fog.

When the sea is calm and still,
The seagulls screech happily and
Fly about flapping their wings.
The dog is lazy in the day after
A rough night being vicious.
When the sea is quiet in the afternoon
The sight is quite a thrill.

Jonny Nandakumar (11)
The Garendon High School

The Sea

The sea at night calls out to you
as the moon shines down upon it,
the waves make it seem like it's a blanket of warmth
and calling people into it.

The sea in daylight looks warm and fun
as people stop and play each day,
a crowd gathers there as it's a place to stay.

The blues and greens look like soap upon
I'd like to dine with seaweed and fish to feast upon
wouldn't it be fine?

As the tide goes in and out
each time it leaves us treasures to find
like rock pools, crabs and different shells
to which we take away
you can smell the salt of the water's breeze
as it hits your lips to which they dry up
so tight you have to lick your lips!

Kelly Spiby (11)
The Garendon High School

The Silver-Lined Sea

Crash! The sea is an angry bear,
Desperately trying to tackle the rugged rocks.
He roars and bellows, but the cliffs don't care,
The cliffs are strong and tall, they can take his knocks.

Realising this, the bear hunts smaller prey,
Like innocent people that lie in the bay,
He then pulls at their feet and draws them in . . .
So they go for a quick swim.

The small waves lap on the shore,
The bear is going.

Laurence Vardaxglou (11)
The Garendon High School

The Sea - Tropical

The sea, like individual crystals,
Gleaming in the blinding sun.
So pretty, so blue,
I can't draw my eyes to my love.

The sound in the shells,
Is the same sound as the waves,
Gently rolling onto my feet.
The sounds of the pan-tropical birds,
Are music to my sunburnt ears.

My love,
Can't you see the darting fish,
And the dolphins leaping up so high?
No, your dull eyes see nothing.

If you wish not to stay on this island,
I don't care.
This is the world I love,
And nothing can take away its pride and beauty.

Rachel Blanchard (11)
The Garendon High School

The Sea

T ethered to a post,
H e squirms and struggles,
E ven the tall rocks cower away!

S ensing sickening danger,
E merging from the oceans deep,
A n enormous wave crashes against the rocks.

K illing like a huntsman,
I mage of white spray,
L icking the broken rocks,
L ulling to the sound,
S eemingly the gulls in the sky.

Scott Lacey (11)
The Garendon High School

The Sea

The sea is a wild eagle,
Brilliant and blue,
He sweeps across the beach,
Searching for food.

His wings widespread,
He searches for a fight.

Crash! A lightning strike
Like a bullet from a height,
Rapid waves,
Wide, wide whirlpools.

But soon enough,
The great bird shall cool.

Thomas Neill (11)
The Garendon High School

Sea Rap

The sea is full of sounds,
White horses all around,
Hear people playin' in the background.

It's draggin' me under,
Waves sound like thunder,
Poseidon is hidin'
I find myself risin'.

People are as dumb as sheep,
When other people see me and weep,
No one comes to help 'cause they're cryin' on the kelp.

The lifeguard can't see me,
But the sea set me free.

Charlie Hague (11)
The Garendon High School

The Sea

The sea, so secretive, silent, stormy,
A place which could tell a thousand stories.

The sea, so many colours from blue, green to grey,
Silently flowing backwards and forwards into a bay.

Seagulls shrieking, swooping, seeking food,
Seals, squid and shrimps think them quite rude.

Down in the depths of the world unknown,
Fish, sharks and whales all together, yet alone.

We'll never really know all that lies therein,
But it's very much a part of the world we live in.

James Langran (11)
The Garendon High School

The Sea

T he sea was like a dark blanket.
H overing sand swished on top of the sea.
E ndless sights were seen.

S ightseeing scenes appeared as the sun disappeared.
E xhausted travellers relaxed as the moon appeared.
A t long last, morning rose and fishy, fresh smells were smelt.

Gemma Brailsford (12)
The Garendon High School

School Poem

If you think school is cool then you must be a fool.
Do you like fighting, or do you like writing?
Bullies call people names like those poor children; Harry and James.
They will push you in the river and it will make you shiver.

Sam Potter (11)
The Garendon High School

Fireworks

Up in the air,
The fireworks soar.
They *bang, crash*,
Sparkle and roar.

A crowd is watching
The magnificent sight,
They gaze in awe
And jump with fright.

Yellow, red, green and blue,
Orange, pink and purple too.
'Ooh' and 'Ahh' cries everyone,
A grand finale, soon they're gone!

Emily Shaw (11)
The Garendon High School

The Fantastic Sea

The sea
Is an honour to me
As it is so far away
The boats and the fish
And the tropical dish
I will have it all each day

The sea is like a giant pool
Full of fish all swimming in their school
With the waves that break
That make the rocks shake

But then I wake
To discover it was all a dream.

Sophie Mayfield (12)
The Garendon High School

Autumn

Autumn when the days are shorter
makes me think of when I was younger
collecting conkers on the way to school
and as I walked to the swimming pool.
How I loved those days
with those carefree ways.

Rachel Edney (11)
The Garendon High School

Old Tom

My cat Tom
Has three legs
I'm sure he thinks they're pegs
He walks around my feet all day
Seems to have a lot to say
Miaow, miaow, miaow
Please come on
And feed me now.

I walk into the lounge
Guess what? He's asleep
In my spot
Come on Old Tom, get off there
You've been there all day
It's not fair.
Come on Old Tom, it's time to go out
You really need to run about
The 15-year-old you are, you really are my star.

Matthew Ayris (13)
The Grange School

Music Is Loud

I like music
How can I use it?
I like it loud
My head's in the clouds

The louder the better
Put it in a letter
Write me a song
And send it along

Do you like it?
Shall I write it?
Write you a song
And send it along.

Gary Bright (11)
The Grange School

Leaves

The fallen leaves
On the ground.
When you walk on them
They make
A crunching sound.

When you're playing out,
The nights are getting darker.

The wind is blowing
Against the trees
They go *whoosh*
As the leaves fall down.

Brett Bailey (12)
The Grange School

Fish In The Sea

Fish in the sea
What do you see?
I am a fish
What do you think I see?

I think you see sharks
Fighting in the sea
That is correct
But that is not all I see

Try again
But try to be me
I think you see seals
Playing with all that they see

Yes, yes. You are starting to see
That is good - but what else may I see?
What about the sea
How mean can she be?

I can't tell for this is my home
And this is where I'll always be.

Matthew Snow (14)
The Grange School

What Can You See?

Boy in the minibus
What can you see?

I see the country road
Stretching out in front of me.

Cows on the left
Horses and tractors to the right.

Cars in the front and behind
Their lights on in the night.

Darren George (12)
The Grange School

My Home

I like the cold, freezing ice
Skating boots
Seeing the pond
Makes me happy

We move to bowling
It gets hard
I am good
But you are better

I go to the car boot on Sundays
We go to the ice rink
It is cold, I am good
But I have to hold
I am not told but,
You are told

I go to my foster carer's
I love this too
It is fun
But I like this
Better than anyone.

Daniel Masters (12)
The Grange School

What Do You Hear? What Do You See?

Beaver in the lodge, what do you hear?
I see a dragonfly looking for me.

Snake in the grass, what do you see?
I see an ant being silly.

Wolf in the pack, what do you hear?
I hear a bush baby having a beer.

Parrot in the jungle, what do you hear?
I hear a crocodile whispering in my ear.

Ewan Bellamy (10)
The Grange School

Hawk In The Sky What Can You See?

Rolling hills speeding past
A horse or two cantering across a grassy field
A mouse running to avoid the stampede
Then the trees of the forest
The occasional screech of an owl swooping for its prey
Now, over a motorway, cars in a long traffic jam
Sliding into the horizon like a long snake
Now a town with rows of houses
Children playing o the road
Fields again, some sheep, a farmhouse
A bullet flying up
All I see now is the ground zooming towards me.

Alex Franklin (15)
The Grange School

I Wish I Had A Brain

Because school is so lame,
Because I always take the blame,
People call me names,
When I play the game.

When can I find my brain?
Is it down the lane?
Is it in the classroom?
No, it's down the drain.

Now I have a brain
I no longer take the blame,
Shall I give it a name?
The name of my brain is David Blane.

Michael Shaw (12)
The Grange School

I Was Afraid

I got in the van
We drove to Rutland Water
I was afraid
I got in the canoe
I hope I don't sink
I was afraid
I got in the kayak
I fell out
I laughed and laughed
I was not afraid.

Jack Makepeace (9)
The Grange School

Spanish Life

Old Spanish men talking politics
Young at heart, still football lunatics
Sangria sitting next to their
Old fashioned walking sticks

I can count in Spanish from one to six
Bullfighters fighting with wooden sticks
Women watching, feeling sick
Spanish life, oh so rich.

Darryl Chambers (15)
The Grange School

A Poem About A Zoo

Python in the zoo, what can he see?
People walking by, eating ice cream
Toys in their hands, furry animals to remember us by
Red shirts like blood making them think of food.
Python in the zoo, what can he hear?
Vibration of people banging on the glass.

David Haman (14)
The Grange School

Once There Was A Bullfight

Once there was a bullfight
The picadors stabbed the bull
In the back of the head and then ran out

Then the matador came in
He did the fancy stuff
With a red cape
The bull gored him in the guts and killed him

1-0 to the bull.

Edmund Maile (13)
The Grange School

Scaly The Scary Monster

His metallic eyes as round as a satellite
His nose as squidgy as a trifle
Ears as sharp as a glistening pinpoint
Stinking and wet as ripened wee
Hands black and sticky as melted tar
Body scaly as a slimy fish
Giving out smoke like a burning fire.

Jason Johnson (13)
The Grange School

Trees

Trees are big and strong
And they grow all the day long
They are covered in bark and leaves
Trees are used to make the paper
I'm writing on
The wood is used for making things
Like tables and chairs
Trees are good for climbing up.

Sam Duffield (14)
The Grange School

The Match

We played
Oakham Rugby team
I was feeling very keen
I put on my kit
And I felt very fit

We ran onto the pitch
Lee got a stitch
The whistle blew to begin
We all wanted to win

We got six tries
I am telling no lies
Our fans were all cheering
And some began to sing

The end of the match came
Oh what a good game
We all had fun
And were happy we won.

Stevie Newbold (14)
The Grange School

I Like Noise

I like noise,
The huffing,
The puffing,
And buffing of a train.

The teaming,
And splashing,
And streaming of the rain.

The clashing,
The bashing,
And smashing of the plates.

Dean Gray (12)
The Grange School

The Fish

The fish was in the water
Snooping with his mates he was a crusion
Not a scratch on him he was speeding like a leopard
Looking for his prey
When suddenly he saw some maggots
Other fish were eating them
He saw four maggots together
Like a mother with her newborn child
Could it be the man they talk about in his green cupboard
Waiting to pull me in on string?
But I took it
Next thing I knew
I was in a net.

Liam Barber (14)
The Grange School

My Garden

My garden is bright and green
It's the best garden I've ever seen,
The sun is bright and yellow,
The wind is nice and mellow,
I have a nice mango tree,
It's there for me and you to see,
It has a lot of space,
My garden is a really lovely place.

Marshyane Allen (12)
The Grange School

Poems!

I've been asked to write a poem,
The reason I don't know why,
So little inspiration
As time just passes me by.

I haven't written a poem since primary school
I would really like to keep it that way.
I'm not Carol Ann Duffy,
Let's not pretend otherwise
And that's the way it should stay.

People keep on talking,
As thoughts swirl around in my head.
What will I have for tea?
When can I go to bed?

Will this lesson ever end?
I'd really like to know.
I am no poet,
Yes, I do know it.
So if it rhymes,
It is no friend of mine!

Sarah Fowler (16)
The Rutland College

Superstition

Why do I always see
one lone magpie fly overhead,
Or two swoop by and one drops
                                      dead?

Nicole Baines (16)
The Rutland College

Lee

Up in the sky, I see your face,
Up in the sky, save me a place.
You're an angel,
You're a star.
I know you're safe wherever you are.

You didn't say goodbye,
You didn't get a chance,
You were a fighter,
You were full of life,
You brought to this world,
More than you can imagine.
One day we'll all meet up,
One day we'll all be together . . .
One day everything will be normal again.

Kayleigh Smith (17)
The Rutland College

Black And Blue

I sit and hide as the car draws near,
She pulls up to the drive, she can feel my fear.
My name is called, she shouts and raves,
As I sit here cuddling Ted.

She starts to hit me, makes me cry,
She makes me feel like I want to die.
She taunts me and beats me and pulls me hair,
I scream for help but no one's there.

I sit here in shame with my head held low,
With cuts and bruises form head to toe.
What did I do to deserve this?
All I want is a hug and a kiss.

Emily Culpin (16)
The Rutland College

Anti-Social

I don't wanna talk to you
I don't care where you're from,
'Cause I'm anti-social
Why should I give a damn?

I like standing here,
Away from the rest of the world
'Cause I'm anti-social.

My problems are my own,
That's how it should be.
I don't wanna hear it,
You're all dead to me

'Cause I'm anti-social,
I sometimes feel a pain.
It hangs on to me,
Shadows my every move.

No. I don't need you
I never had despised something
As müch as this,
'Cause I'm anti-social
I confront myself constantly.
The trouble is though, I never win.

Ben Knight (16)
The Rutland College

Brother V Brother

It's brother against brother,
Blood against blood,
Vision's all blurred,
By tears stained blood-red;
It's man against son,
Now the fight has begun,
One shot leads to another,
They don't care how many are dead.

It's faith against faith,
Which keeps the fires raging,
It's ignorance and fear,
That fans the flames of hatred;
It's barbarity that forces the door open,
To shoot in front of his family.
An innocent man, for what they say is sacred.

It's country against country,
That keeps the world divided;
It's the government against the people,
That keeps the wars going on,
That sets father against son
And brother against brother,
When we should all be able to live in peace,
And still the killing goes on.

Gemma Willison (17)
The Rutland College

Love's Strife

Entering through the big white door,
I see the children playing on the floor,
Building blocks and Barbie dolls scattering,
While gleeful parents are chattering.

Will I ever be like this? I ask,
Getting over him is such a task.
They say they come and go,
Like walking through fresh white snow.

World problems, the starving, the poor,
I have my own worries; I'm lonely to the core.
Caring for someone so intensely,
When it ends it hurts immensely.

Someone else will come along,
Like the beginning of a new love song.
He will be out of my life
And it will be an end to all this strife.

So although one love had ended
And I feel like I have been suspended,
I'm keeping my head held high,
Trying my hardest not to cry.

Julia Penfold (16)
The Rutland College

And -

and -
squiggles on the page
red - yellow - green - blue

jackandjill come tumbling
down - the - hill and

lollipops and buttons

sheep bleating in - the - field
eating grass and the red - train
chugging
   along

and sophieandabbi come skipping
from hopscotch and snakesandladders and

it's winter
and
   the
      snowman

off the wall
humpty
    dumpty.

Katie Almond (16)
The Rutland College

Ideas

I am sitting here writing a poem
But I don't know what to put
Why am I doing this?
I'm sat here stuck in a rut.

I'm thinking of different ideas,
To put down on my page
Maybe a poem about love,
When your heart is kept in a cage.

Should the theme be about crime?
We've got so much violence on our streets.
I could write a poem about humour
Or how bullying starts with just one rumour.

There are so many ideas
For my poem that I could put,
At least I've got some themes
So I'm not stuck in a rut!

Harriet Moody (16)
The Rutland College

Playing The Violin With No Strings

One day I heard a poem,
From an idol that's in the sky,
He believed a rose was beautiful, growing from concrete,
Even if the petals were dull,
You still marvel at the rose pushing its way through the concrete,
Does this mean a spider is beautiful?
Building a silky web,
Or perhaps moss looking dull growing on the wall,
Although never to be seen to fall,
I see hope in the world of people pushing harder to get through,
Never to be dull of its puny petals,
Just shine through like you.

Christian Aleksov (16)
The Rutland College

Caesar

Sit down children,
As I tell you a story,
A story of a ruler filled with a passionate hate,
A black fire spitting green embers of hate within his heart
This man you ask?
Julius Caesar
Who infected the city of Rome with fear back in the time of
BCE
Despising Christians for one reason or another
Who would (dare) speak the name of might and saviour
Sending his army of Red and Gold-draped hounds,
Out on the vulnerable midnight hour
In protest to the Christian faith
Religious families forced to flee
From the interrupted line of 'deliver us from evil'
Fires tearing through the homes of the people who refuse to
Surrender their beliefs
Logs emitted with hate and anger,
Embers scattering wildly with short, sharp crackles
Ignited further by Caesar's deadly black hate.

Terri Lynch (16)
The Rutland College

A Poem About The World

Millions of people die each day,
It doesn't have to be this way,
No more hunger, famine and war,
Make it stop, we don't want any more.

Let's make the world a better place,
Let's put some smiles on our face,
Millions of people die each day,
It doesn't have to be this way.

Loretta Johnson (16)
The Rutland College

Netahne (Flying)
(Dedicated to Aram Khatchaturian)

Music.
A universal language of sound.

My favourite piece from years ago.
It seems so simple now.
And so we begin (Khatchaturian and I),
In E flat major.
He is speaking to me through his composition.
A poignant melody.

The black and white keys are in symbiosis now,
As we approach the crescendo.
The notes are dancing off the page,
Ivan you sing so well!
Moving from the bass to the treble clef.
Two slurs towards the end.

When the last chord dies away,
The connection is fractured.
Until we play again.
Encore Ivan!

Coby Richardson   (17)
The Rutland College

Sky

The stars are humming sweetly
To the mountains and the streams
The sleeping world lies helpless
Entranced by moonlit dreams.

The crumpled sky grows drowsy
Beneath the breathless, heavy night
The dreams are slowly twisting
Softy glowing, out of sight.

Tori Thomas (16)
The Rutland College

Nanna

Your eyes still burn with fiery youth,
> though youth has long since died,
They proudly gaze across the room,
> those eyes that never lied.

Your wrinkled hands still poised with grace,
> though now are deathly cold,
Your trophies of the bygone days,
> which young men longed to hold.

A popular girl in photos,
> though now your friends are dead,
Lost memories of those happy years,
> alive still in your head.

But from your old and caring eyes,
> that young girl stares at me,
Despite your slowly fading flame,
> it is her that I see.

Charlotte Wilce (17)
The Rutland College

Suicidal

I am here, I am there, I am nowhere
I used to be someone, nobody is better
Ever since the time my life seemed to fade away
Now all I see are empty faces and empty words

They echo in my head, but I still feel nothing
No emotions, nothing there to feel
Compassion, sadness, anger, happiness - they mean nothing to me
They faded away a long time ago

Just like me, just like my sanity
Now I have nothing, things don't seem as important
Like my life, that's the thing I'll be glad to get rid of the most.

Sarah Bruce (16)
The Rutland College

I Know How She Feels . . .

they say.
She stares at the ceiling contemplating
her life, discussing in her mind a direction of
freedom from the pain.
A delicate embrace,
an attempt of providing a temporary
comfort yet still she cries a tear for
every lie heaved upon her,
a tear for every cruelty hurled at her,
a tear for herself.
Why not?
Nobody else will shed one for me,
her mind whirls.
Why does it matter?
Every relief is temporary
every hurt returns,
every hit of sadness is stronger all the time,
mounting up,
unsteadily,
ready to fall, crushing every delicate
uplifting idea she holds on so tight to.
I know how she feels, they say.
But do they?

Hazel Johns (16)
The Rutland College

First Love

Their faces were lit with the glow of a lifetime of stars,
Lights to represent the heroes of present and past,
The clouds rested lazily in the sky so still,
Waiting for Cupid to fire at his will.

'Banquet, fireworks and love at first sight'
The flyer answered the lonesome plight;
To wait for love or do not look at all,
Or to take a chance and risk a fall?

Two such people looking for love,
Were lit by the glow of the stars above,
And Cupid saw what others could not;
Two people, so different,
Diverse backgrounds and lives,
But spirits full of passion make a love that never dies.

The match was seen by the king of love,
The stage was set with the glow from above,
The crowds did part and their eyes did lock,
And love swept through them like the tide at a dock.

At that moment two hearts became one,
United in the feeling that had overcome;
A feeling of warmth, tenderness and love,
And Cupid's happiness rained down from above.

Hannah D'Cruz (16)
The Rutland College

My Poetic Catastrophe

I sit here in class,
Staring through the glass
Summer pouring through the window,
I'd rather be out there, that I know.

Write a poem the teacher drones,
The class's mood drops like blown-over traffic cones.
Oh no, I think, *not again,*
I'd done it before, now and then!

The words never rhyme,
And they take so much time.
It feels like a curse,
With every ill put-together verse.

Lexis, simile, parenthesis,
I think, *why am I doing this?*
Description, alliteration, pun,
I'd rather be out there having fun.

Then suddenly, without advance,
I take my chance.
To the paper I pour out my head,
'OK, stop now,' the teacher said.

This is the result of my poetic test,
As I slapped it down on the teacher's desk.
I'm the boy who couldn't write poetry,
Hence my poetic catastrophe.

Russell Kent-Payne (16)
The Rutland College

. . . And Anxiety Is?

Looks like
    I've past my best
And now I've reached my worst
Take a left turn
(And you'll come to nowhere)
Can't find
    the words to say
What's been built up inside
Go on ahead
(I'll meet you there)

Cos I want it and I need it
To be the same as it was before
You don't know it yet, and I can never show you it
I just can't take this s**t anymore!
(Or words to that effect).

(I need something to occupy my mind)
Too tired to . . . think
Too tired to . . . care
Too tired to . . . sleep?
And I'm too tired to dream

I said it
    once before
But I'll say it again
(Maybe I will be fine tomorrow)
Am I deceiving myself
    hanging onto my only wish
(Of undreamt dreams that won't be drowned in sorrow)?

Graham Turner (16)
The Rutland College

Moving

An empty room,
I'm ten years away,
To when I was small,
My toys filled this space,
This lonely space.

Each dent in the skirting,
Each scratch on the green wall,
Tells my life in this house,
Forgotten times,
The happy and the sad.

The drawings behind the wardrobe,
Hidden from my mum;
The games under my bed,
From when my friends came to play,
All stuck in past memories.

But now I feel lost,
As my life is packed away,
Past and present,
All moved to the future,
An uncertain future.

My possessions will not belong,
When in someone else's room;
My memories will change,
And eventually fade,
As I struggle to remember,
My life at number twenty-one.

Kirsty Chuter (16)
The Rutland College

War

Why do we have to fight?
Why do people end up on the floor?
Why do we use violence?
What is war?

Is it conflict?
Is it fighting?
Is it violent
Or is it meant to be in writing?

Why do we have to argue?
What is at the core?
Why do we use weapons?
What is war?

Is it reason?
Is it truthless?
Is it fair
Or is it just ruthless?

What *is* war?

Katie Folwell (16)
The Rutland College

I'm Never Sarcastic . . .

If I'm absolutely honest,
Pop music is the best.
Without telling a lie,
Dance music seriously rocks.

If I were a politician,
Hitler would be my idol.
With homicide as my hobby,
I'd love to persecute the Jews.

As the world's greatest believer in religion,
I fear the Devil.
Since I pray every night
Perhaps the Messiah will return.

I'm never sarcastic,
I would never write a sarcastic poem.
Sarcasm isn't the lowest form of wit
And I love writing poetry.

Dominic Tomes (16)
The Rutland College

I Am Not What I Am

I am a sweet trout, gliding swiftly through the radiant sky
I am a sombre rose, dying calmly to the bitter wind
I am a calm storm, slowly awaiting a melancholy outburst
I am the sturdy Hoover Dam, holding back a lake of emotions
I am a red monkey, passionately embracing the lofty branch
I am a spring crow, softly weeping dewdrops onto lush grass
I am a rogue wasp, unwilling to cause immense pain
I am a busy fly, often appearing everywhere in my brief life
I could be any of these
However
I am not what I am.

James Barlow (14)
Vale Of Catmose College

A Moment In Time Poem

The two towers slid silently erect again,
the planes propelling backwards
and lives being saved.
In the whisper of the hushed wind,
the copious workers of Hadrian's wall
un-lift vast stone bricks and un-set concrete.
England and Scotland become one again.
In the pop of your gum,
the ghostly remains of the Titanic reappear.
The lights flickering slowly on again
and sailing back towards the port.
As a heart beats it was world-stoppingly announced
that the second World War was over.
In the deathly excuse for a murderer's actions,
the Queen's crown is un-lifted from her head
and she becomes a princess again.
As you draw a breath, the fire of London shrinks again
and becomes a tiny flickering spark.

Vicki Potter (12)
Vale Of Catmose College

Lost Sheep

I am a sickly smile, always happy but sometimes false.
I am a secretive house, enclosing my contents from goggling eyes.
I am the content sun, watching peacefully but never joining in.
I am the scatter-brained cook that always spoils the broth.
I am a forgotten dream, never reaching its goal.
I am a malicious rumour, always causing more trouble than intended.
I am a withered weed in a bed of beautiful roses.
I am a disturbed photograph shoved to the bottom of the pile.
I am a dying star trying to hold on.
I am an unlit candle, one day I will shine.
I am a lost sheep, trying to think for myself.
I am everything to me, yet
I am nothing to you.

Sophie Arnold (14)
Vale Of Catmose College

Life

I am the content statue thinking quietly
amongst the hideous noises of the night.
I am the happy, light summer's rain
trickling down through the hazardous stars.
I am the sour but sweet volcano
waiting to release my fear.
I am the lonely island seeking messages
from the outside world.
I am the tangy nettle growing angrier
ready for anything that comes my way.
I am the silent wolf
deadly in my thinking
I am the calm barracuda
glistening like the water in which it swims.
I am the angry bird fleeing my home
inspecting new forests and making it fit for my family.
I am all the pains of this world and the next
but yet all of the joys as well.

Daniel Goodwin (14)
Vale Of Catmose College

Trophies, Rings, Glasses

When ink has run out in a pen, does it feel like it has died?
Do chairs feel lonely as they are tucked under a dark table?
Are clouds moving because of the wind or is it because
they are taking part in a race?
As wood is burnt, does it scream for help?
Do trophies feel the same happiness as the proud person who won it?
Do the expensive-looking Versace dresses enjoy being photographed
on a wooden model, or would they prefer to be worn for more than
just one glorious hour?
Can a wedding ring tell when divorce is on the way?
Do glasses need eyes to see?
Are gravestones quivering as they look down to the
black depths below?

Caroline Kirstein (14)
Vale Of Catmose College

Volcano

The mountain god stands viewing its kingdom,
deciding its future for the island.
Tempting fate, seeing how far he can reach
without destroying too much.
The flaming lava scorches the sea as it erupts
over the side, engulfing its victims in a blanket of flames.
The deafening rumbles send fear to people's hearts
as he laughs at them fleeing before him.
The birds circle the top as if guarding the golden killer,
watching the devastation.
The sea desperately spits at its challenger,
forcing it back to his home.
But even if it does stand victorious,
the volcano's done its damage.
Its hard cheeks dimple into a cheery smile
as it lays back down to sleep.

Katie Burton (14)
Vale Of Catmose College

Reversing Time

In the strike of a match,
The haunting spectre of a deceased lord, pale and wispy,
reconvenes to its former self.
As fast as a rock falling to Earth,
fading slabs of death dwindle into the shadowed, ghostly mist.
At the rip of a page,
ancient ruins dwelling in ominous, black, thick fog
revert into their splendoured rich selves.
In the scratch of a quill,
the cold phantom of Da Vinci's masterpiece, terribly perfected,
retraces its steps back to the brush and becomes
a spirit of its dreadful self.

From taunting myth to legend, to savage tale to
word of mouth, to the reckless phenomenon.

Pippa Gray (12)
Vale Of Catmose College

The Iraqi Children

It's not their fault that they must suffer
but if not them, then surely another
hear the crying, screaming silence
and all of this because of violence
a mind of sickness
a sea of blood
they gain no help from God above
we can't do much but watch in pain
like a sad, unhealed, burning flame
see the fear within their eyes
walking on eggshells, living in lies
switch off a light, say goodnight
and think of them, they're out of sight
we can't say it's over, it's in the past
when kids are dying - dying fast.

Yasmin Mulligan (15)
Vale Of Catmose College

When Time Went Into Reverse

The crumbly, bent trees twist down into the ground
in the time it takes for a tent zip to be undone.
Goliath the giant lies like a three-acre woodland area,
as the smooth pebble jerks and then it took a flash of a camera
for it to reach David's hand.
The London Bridge is being unbuilt, the wires and materials
lie still on the ground back in the days of a quiet place.
Gently the sword glides in like a waxed surfboard
against the sea waves.
Into the rock, to where the sword stood before being pulled out
by the Lord's right hand.
In the murmur of an underground train the busy,
busting emerald-green globe is being gently dismantled
by the worn, warm, wrinkled hands of God.

Hannah Arnold (12)
Vale Of Catmose College

Re: Verse

As swift as a dolphin leaping out of the waves, clumps of curly hair
floated gently back up to the young girl's head, like small
drifting clouds.
With a flourish, the hairdresser snapped the blades of his scissors
together, put them back in his pocket and looked attentively
at the girl's face in the mirror.
In the beating of a heart, like a slippery snake,
the thread rapidly slithered back up through the whirring cogs
and wheels of the sewing machine. Spinning wildly, the reel soon
filled with cotton, leaving the two limp pieces of material to fall
separately to the floor.
In the click of a flashing camera, reflections of the sky soon
disappeared as large, shiny puddles quickly evaporated.
Huge spots of rain lashed back up into the clouds like thousands
of shards of shattered glass.
Faster than a flashing streak of bright lightning, the huge liner
slowly regained its balance as it separated from the treacherous
iceberg. Like a tree at Christmas, the lights all came on and music
could be heard as the Titanic sailed majestically across the water.
In the quiet beat of a ticking clock, blood trickled up the hands
and feet. The ragged open wounds quickly closed over as the
nails were removed and the crown of thorns lifted.
Carefully the body was taken down from the cross.

Georgia Gibson-Smith (12)
Vale Of Catmose College

A Question

When you turn a light on, does it really shine or does it just work?
When the sky turns grey is it frowning?
Is a calculator more intelligent than its batteries?
Does the stork ever get lost?
Is a spider's web a structure or a home?
When the rose dies does the love die too?
Does a question really want an answer?

Lauren McCombie Smith (14)
Vale Of Catmose College

Picture

It tells the most amazing stories, but never moves its mouth.
It is unique, only one of a treasured kind.
It will last forever, it will never rot or fade
and can be passed from ancestor to ancestor.
It is full of irreplaceable memories which will make you laugh or cry.
Its distinguished eyes follow you around the room
like a shadow of doubt, unavoidable.
It hangs, perfectly still, unable to get up and walk away
from the penetrating stares.
It will always be treasured as a part of the past, it will remind you
of important times and the love shown through it will never die.
Its self-consciousness grows every day from the long, hard stares
it receives from passers by who can't help but talk about it
and criticise.
It tells us not to be afraid of the future, as if by looking at it
helps us understand it may just be as fun as the past.
When looking at it, memories of glorious times play on your mind,
making a smile spread across a humble face.

Kelly Pridmore (14)
Vale Of Catmose College

I Am . . .

I am the tiny snapdragon, I envy the rose's beauty
I am the slippery squid only to come out on peaceful Sunday
I am the caring dad, protecting my newborn phoenix children
I am the fierce sea storm; you can see the glistening emerald
I am the giant spine of the hot and dry savannah
I am the scavenging condor circling my prey above
                    the big wide reservoir
I am the huge redwood standing up looking down on the others
              wearing my skull and crossbones bandanna

Am I any of these?
No I am none of these
I am what I believe.

Luke Chase (15)
Vale Of Catmose College

Sheep

In hilly Wales I found and followed
a path of wool only to find
shorn sheep gathered in the fields of grass.
A wave of flies congregate round
their smell attracts.
Just then, while I was admiring these animals
with teeth to eat anything
an angry farmer counted his sheep.
He stared at me and bellowed,
'Hey boy'o, get yer sheep off my mountain.'
I think he had one too many of these lazy animals.
A blur of confusion came upon me.
Why he shouted at me was hazy.
I had no sheep
and if I did
how would I find it in this sea of clouds?
The angry Welshman charged at me powerfully
I escaped, worried,
but not of what he would have done to me
but what he does with his sheep.
The slaughterhouse is near.

Christopher Young (14)
Vale Of Catmose College

What I Am

I am the mutinous waterfall outraged by winter
I am the eagle hailing down onto a mouse
I am the overheated glacier fighting for life
I am the mythological moss that creeps the earth
I am the obvious chameleon showing off
I am the razor strands of grass with a pink colour
I am the glassy desert that cries endlessly
I am the abstract snake disguised in dense bushes
I am only what I am, only I am nothing more.

Tom Hampson (14)
Vale Of Catmose College

Pelican Hats And Jamaican Slugs

I am a frosty Monday morning,
my sparkling crystals showered over green.
I am cheeks, magenta and glowing.
I am a slug whose sticky, shiny body is glassy under Jamaica's sun.

I am a Venus flytrap volcano,
snapping shut my hungry jaws,
breathing out my fiery orange roar.
I am a squid's great grandfather, resting peacefully in foggy water,
watching rainbow clouds swim slowly past.
I am a pelican hat, beak reaching out, casting a cooling shadow.

Only I can decide what I want to be,
I make myself what I am,
I am me.

Rosie Hind (14)
Vale Of Catmose College

Jungle

In the jungle, it seems there's nothing but celebrities
flirting, laughing and crying.
Rare animals that you've never seen keeping an eye on the invaders.
Bulky green trees with lazy vines like feather boas.
So many rare plants never seen before.
Homesick houseplants like someone who has left home.
Animals need a change of scenery after being bored of colour green.
The rain beats down on the canopy of the great green mass that
spreads across many miles.
Trees demolished by the cruel roaring chainsaw hacking
through their branches.
Monkeys swinging past the leaves, skimming the bark
of the few surviving trees.

Simon Brown (14)
Vale Of Catmose College

Greed

A fountain of lies falling on deaf ears,
growing intently over the years,
like a magpie, it snatches at a hint of gold,
a wave of hunger - never to grow old,
green envy shines through the minor cracks,
greed can't hide behind these indifferent masks,
spreading over us like some infectious disease,
possessions and money are all it needs.

Every one of us holds this sin,
but do we own it from when we begin
or is it just something we learn from others,
passed on through generations to our fathers and mothers?
This power corrupts the sweetest of kinds,
brainwashing our busy, individual minds,
but still there is hope down our family tree,
one may break from this dynasty.

We need to learn to keep the truth and morals,
not to follow each other like naïve fish in their shoals,
but this hungry lioness is creeping up close,
soon to devour us with her deadly dose.

Emily Wilce (14)
Vale Of Catmose College